✴ At a Glance

Paragraphs

✳ At a Glance

Paragraphs

THIRD EDITION

Lee Brandon
Mt. San Antonio College

Houghton Mifflin Company   *Boston*   *New York*

Publisher: Patricia A. Coryell
Senior Sponsoring Editor: Lisa Kimball
Senior Development Editor: Judith Fifer
Editorial Associate: Peter Mooney
Project Editor: Shelley Dickerson
Manufacturing Coordinator: Chuck Dutton
Senior Marketing Manager: Annamarie Rice
Marketing Assistant: Andrew Whitacre

Cover image: © Ablestock

Acknowledgment:

Excerpt from "When Cupid Aims at the Workplace" by Harvey R. Meyer.
Reprinted by permission, *Nation's Business,* Vol. 86, Issue 7. July 1998.
Copyright 1998, U.S. Chamber of Commerce.

Printed in the U.S.A.

Library of Congress Control Number: 2004115527

ISBN: 0-618-54227-2

23456789 – MP – 09 08 07 06 05

✳ Contents

Handbook   172

✳ Preface

At a Glance: Paragraphs is the second-level book in the *At a Glance* series. Along with *At a Glance: Sentences, At a Glance: Essays,* and *At a Glance: Reader,* it meets the current need for succinct, comprehensive, and up-to-date textbooks that students can afford. All four books provide basic instruction, exercises, and writing assignments at the designated level, as well as support material for instructors. *At a Glance: Sentences* and *At a Glance: Paragraphs* include a transition to the next level of writing, while *At a Glance: Paragraphs, At a Glance: Essays,* and *At a Glance: Reader* end with a handbook, to which students can refer for help with sentence-level issues or for problems with mechanics. *At a Glance: Reader* presents brief writing instruction and thirty sources for reading-related writing. Each book in the *At a Glance* series can be used alone, with one of the other *At a Glance* books, or with another textbook. Two or more *At a Glance* books can be shrink-wrapped and delivered at a discount.

✳ Comprehensive Coverage

Focusing on paragraph writing, *At a Glance: Paragraphs* begins with a chapter on how to read critically and write summaries and critiques. It continues with two chapters on prewriting techniques, first-draft writing, revising, and editing—each phase illustrated with student examples. The book then presents ten patterns of paragraph writing, with a chapter devoted to each: narration, description, exemplification, analysis by division, process analysis, cause and effect, classification, comparison and contrast, definition, and argument.

The final chapter provides a bridge to the writing of essays and includes examples and strategies for expanding paragraphs into short essays. *At a Glance: Paragraphs* concludes with a handbook that addresses sentence-level issues (subjects and verbs, fragments, coordination and subordination, and so on); specific verb, pronoun, and modifier problems; punctuation; capitalization; and spelling.

✳ Instructional Approach

The instruction in *At a Glance: Paragraphs* is concise and direct. Each of Chapters 4 through 13 presents a writing strategy for a particular pattern, followed by an annotated student example, a professional example with questions for students to answer, an exercise that gives students practice in organizing the pattern, topic selection (reading-related, cross-curricular, career-related, and general topics) for writing such paragraphs or short essays, and a summary of guidelines specific to the pattern.

Changes for this edition include the following:

- the chapter on reading-related writing, including instructions on how to underline, annotate, outline, and write summaries and critiques, moved to beginning
- fourteen new reading selections
- a new list of cross-curricular topics for each of Chapters 4 through 13
- an expanded handbook section, including units on diction, sentence variety, and omissions
- a new *At a Glance* student website at http://college.hmco.com/ devenglish/student and other Houghton Mifflin support
- the Writing Process Worksheet

✳ Support Material for Instructors

- *At a Glance* instructor website at http://college.hmco.com/ devenglish/instructor: Answers to exercises; reproducible diagnostic tests and sentence-writing quizzes; sample syllabus to adopt or adapt for different course designs; and PowerPoint slides that can be downloaded and used to enhance classroom instruction.
- *At a Glance* student website at http://college.hmco.com/ devenglish/student: Additional exercises; additional readings; instructions for writing résumés and letters of application.
- Software resources include updated Expressways 5.0 CD-ROM, interactive software that guides students as they write and revise paragraphs and essays; Houghton Mifflin Grammar CD-ROM; and the American Heritage Dictionary CD-ROM.

- Online options include Dolphinville, an online writing center, and SMARTHINKING, live online tutoring and academic support by trained e-instructors.

✳ Acknowledgments

I am profoundly indebted to the following instructors who have reviewed this textbook: Cheyenne Adams, Genesee Community College; Anita Aufiero, Gibbs School; Marilyn Black, Middlesex Community College; Thomas Beverage, Coastal Carolina Community College; Deborah Burson-Smith, Southern University at New Orleans; Joanna B. Chrzanowski, Jefferson Community College; Timothy J. Jones, Oklahoma City Community College; David Lang, Golden Gate University; Phyllis MacCameron, Erie Community College; Kathy Masters, Arkansas State University; Richard Pepp, Massasoit Community College; and Steve Stremmel, American River College. Thanks also to members of the English Department at Mt. San Antonio College.

I deeply appreciate the work of freelance editor Mary Dalton Hoffman; Nancy Benjamin of Books By Design; and my colleagues at Houghton Mifflin: Lisa Kimball, Judith Fifer, Annamarie Rice, Andrew Whitacre, Peter Mooney, and Shelley Dickerson.

I am especially grateful to my family of wife, children and their spouses, and grandchildren for their cheerful, inspiring support: Sharon, Kelly, Erin, Kathy, Michael, Shane, Lauren, Jarrett, and Matthew.

Lee Brandon

✳ Student Overview

This book is designed to help you write better paragraphs. Chapter 1 explains how to read critically and write summaries and critiques of reading selections. Chapters 2 and 3 focus on the writing process itself. You'll discover prewriting techniques to help you get started, and you'll learn ways to develop, revise, and edit your drafts until you produce a polished paragraph.

Each of Chapters 4 through 13 describes a different pattern for developing an effective paragraph. Chapter 4, for instance, is about narration; Chapter 5 is about description; Chapter 6 is about exemplification—that is, the use of examples. All of those chapters include sample paragraphs written by students and professional writers. Throughout, questions and exercises help you practice what you have learned.

Chapter 14 discusses the essay in relation to the paragraph and can help you expand some of your paragraphs into essays. Chapter 14 is followed by a handbook, to which you can refer when you need assistance in grammar, usage, punctuation, and capitalization.

Following are some strategies to help you make the best use of this book and to jump-start the improvement in your writing skills.

1. **Be active and systematic in learning.** Take advantage of your instructor's expertise by being an active participant in class—one who takes notes, asks questions, and contributes to discussion. Become dedicated to systematic learning: determine your needs, decide what to do, and do it. Make learning a part of your everyday thinking and behavior.

2. **Read widely.** Samuel Johnson, a great English scholar, once said he didn't want to read anything by people who had written more than they had read. William Faulkner, a Nobel Prize winner in literature, said, "Read, read, read. Read everything—trash, classics, good and bad, and see how writers do it." Read to learn technique, to acquire ideas, to be stimulated to write. Especially read to satisfy your curiosity and to receive pleasure. If reading is a main component of your course, approach it as systematically as you do writing.

3. **Keep a journal.** Keeping a journal may not be required in your particular class, but whether required or not, jotting down your observations in a notebook is a good idea. Here are some ideas for daily, or almost daily, journal writing:

- Summarize, evaluate, or react to reading assignments.
- Summarize, evaluate, or react to what you see on television and in movies, and to what you read in newspapers and magazines.
- Describe and narrate situations or events you experience.
- Write about career-related matters you encounter in other courses or on the job.

   Your journal entries may read like an intellectual diary, a record of what you are thinking about at certain times. Keeping a journal will help you to understand reading material better, to develop more language skills, and to think more clearly—as well as to become more confident and write more easily so that writing becomes a comfortable, everyday activity. Your entries may also provide subject material for longer, more carefully crafted pieces. The important thing is to get into the habit of writing something each day.

4. **Evaluate your writing skills.** Use the Self-Evaluation Chart inside the front cover of this book to list areas you need to work on. You can add to your lists throughout the entire term. Drawing on your instructor's comments, make notes on matters such as spelling, word choice, paragraph development, grammar, sentences, punctuation, and capitalization. As you master each problem area, you can check it off or cross it out.

   Here is a partially filled out Self-Evaluation Chart, followed by some guidelines for filling out your own.

Self-Evaluation Chart

Spelling/ Word Choice	Paragraph Development	Grammar/ Sentences	Punctuation/ Capitalization
separate	topic	fragment 185	comma after long
a lot	sentence 26	run-on 185	introductory
studying	use specific	parallel	modifier 202
boundary	examples 71	structure 200	periods and
avoid	support 38	subject-verb	commas inside
slang 38		agreement 192	quotation
			marks 204

- *Spelling/Word Choice.* List words marked as incorrectly spelled on your assignments. Master the words on your list and add new words as you accumulate assignments. Also include new, useful words with their brief definitions and comments on word choice, such as avoiding slang, clichés, and vague or general words.
- *Paragraph Development.* List suggestions your instructor made about writing strong topic sentences and attending to matters such as coherence, language, unity, emphasis, and support.
- *Grammar/Sentences.* List problems such as subject-verb agreement, sentence fragments, comma splices, and run-ons. If you tend to begin sentences in the same way or to choose the same patterns, use your chart to remind yourself to vary your sentence patterns and beginnings.
- *Punctuation/Capitalization.* List any problems you encounter with punctuation and capitalization. Because the items in this column may be covered in the handbook at the end of this book, you can often use both rule numbers and page numbers for the references here.

5. **Use the Writing Process Worksheet.** Record details about each of your assignments, such as the due date, topic, length, and form. The worksheet will also remind you of the stages of the writing process: explore, organize, and write. A blank Writing Process Worksheet for you to photocopy for assignments appears on page xx.

6. **Be positive.** All the elements you record in your Self-Evaluation Chart probably are covered in *At a Glance: Paragraphs.* The table of contents, the index, and the correction chart on the inside back cover of the book will direct you to the additional instruction you decide you need.

To improve your English skills, write with freedom, but revise and edit with rigor. Work with your instructor to set attainable goals, and proceed at a reasonable pace. Soon, seeing what you have mastered and checked off your list will give you a sense of accomplishment.

Finally, don't compare yourself with others. Compare yourself with yourself and, as you make progress, consider yourself what you are—a student on the path toward effective writing, a student on the path toward success.

Writing Process Worksheet

Title _____

Name _____ **Due Date** _____

Assignment In the space below, write whatever you need to know about your assignment, including information about the topic, audience, pattern of writing, length, whether to include a rough draft or revised drafts, and whether your paper must be typed.

Stage One **Explore** Freewrite, brainstorm (list), cluster, or take notes as directed by your instructor. Use separate paper if you need more space.

Stage Two **Organize** Write a topic sentence or thesis; label the subject and treatment parts.

Write an outline or a structured list.

Stage Three **Write** On separate paper, write and then revise your paragraph or essay as many times as necessary for coherence, language (usage, tone, and diction), unity, emphasis, support, and sentences (**CLUESS**). Read your work aloud to hear and correct any grammatical errors or awkward-sounding sentences.

Edit any problems in fundamentals, such as capitalization, omissions, punctuation, and spelling (**COPS**).

Reading Effectively and Writing Summaries

Because most college writing assignments are connected with reading, it is worthwhile to consider how to focus thoughtful attention on the written word. Of course, if you know about writing assignments or tests beforehand, your reading can be more concentrated. You should always begin a reading assignment by asking yourself why you are reading that particular material and how it relates to your course work and interests. For example, most selections in this book are presented as ideas to stimulate thought and invite reflective comparisons, to provide material for analysis and evaluation, and to show how a pattern or process of writing can be done effectively. The discussion and critical-thinking questions and activities that follow the selections arise from these purposes. Other questions raised by your instructor or on your own can also direct you in purposeful reading. Consider such questions and activities at the outset. Then, as you read, use strategies that are appropriate for the kind of assignment you are working on. Among the most common strategies are underlining, annotating, and outlining. Used correctly, they will help you attain a critical, receptive, and focused state of mind as you prepare for writing assignments.

✳ Reading for Writing

Underlining

Imagine you are reading a chapter of several pages, and you decide to underline and write in the margins. Immediately, the underlining takes you out of the passive, television-watching frame of mind. You are involved. You are participating. It is now necessary for you to discriminate, to distinguish more important from less important ideas. Perhaps you have thought of underlining as a method designed only to help you with reviewing. That is, when you study the material the next time, you won't have to reread all of it; instead, you can focus on the most important, underlined parts. While you are underlining, you are benefiting from an imposed concentration, because this procedure forces you to think, to focus. Consider the following suggestions for underlining:

1. Underline the main ideas in paragraphs. The most important statement, the topic sentence, is likely to be at the beginning of the paragraph.
2. Underline the support for those main ideas.
3. Underline answers to questions that you bring to the reading assignment. These questions may have come from the end of the chapter, from subheadings that you turn into questions, or from your independent concerns about the topic.
4. Underline only the key words. You would seldom underline all the words in a sentence and almost never a whole paragraph.

Does that fit your approach to underlining? Possibly not. Most students, in their enthusiasm to do a good job, overdo underlining.

The trick is to figure out what to underline. You would seldom underline more than about 30 percent of a passage, although the amount would depend on your purpose and the nature of the material. Following the preceding four suggestions will be useful. Learning more about the principles of sentence, paragraph, and essay organization will also be helpful.

Annotating

Annotating, writing notes in the margins, is related to underlining. You can do it independently, although it usually appears in conjunction with underlining to signal your understanding and to extend your involvement in your reading.

Writing in the margins represents intense involvement because it turns a reader into a writer. If you read material and write something in the margin as a reaction to it, then in a way you have had a conversation with the author. The author has made a statement and you have responded. In fact, you may have added something to the text; therefore, for your purposes you have become a coauthor or collaborator. The comments you make in the margin are of your own choosing, according to your interests and the purpose you bring to the reading assignment. Your response in the margin may merely echo the author's ideas, it may question them critically, it may relate them to something else, or it may add to them.

The comments and marks on the following essay will help you understand the connection between writing and reading. Both techniques—underlining to indicate main and supporting ideas and annotating to indicate their importance and relevance to the task at hand—will enhance reading, thinking, and writing.

Total Institutions

Seymour Feshbach and Bernard Weiner

Total institution encompasses individual (thesis)

A <u>total institution</u> completely <u>encompasses the individual,</u> forming a barrier to the types of social intercourse that occur outside such a setting. Monasteries, jails, homes for the aged, boarding schools, and military academies are a few examples of total institutions.

1. Individual activities in same setting

<u>Total institutions</u> have certain <u>common</u> characteristics. <u>First,</u> the <u>individuals</u> in such environments must <u>sleep, play,</u> and <u>work</u> within the <u>same setting.</u> These are generally segmented spheres of activity in the lives of most individuals, but within a total institution one sphere of activity overlaps with others.

2. All life within group

<u>Second, each phase of life</u> takes place <u>in the company of a large group</u> of others. Frequently, <u>sleeping is done in a barracks,</u> food is served in a cafeteria, and so on. In such activities everyone is treated alike and must perform certain essential tasks. <u>Third, activities</u> in an institution are <u>tightly scheduled</u> according to a <u>master plan,</u> with set times to rise, to eat, to exercise, and to sleep. These institutional characteristics result in a <u>bureaucratic society,</u> which requires the hiring of other people for surveillance. What often results is a split in the groups within an institution into a large, managed group (inmates) and a small supervisory staff. There tends to be <u>great social distance between</u> the <u>groups,</u> who <u>perceive each other according to stereotypes</u> and <u>have</u> severely <u>restricted communications.</u>

3. Activities tightly scheduled

Managed groups and staff at distance

Two worlds —inside and outside

The <u>world of the inmate differs</u> greatly <u>from the outside world.</u> When one enters a total institution, all <u>previous roles,</u> such as father or husband, are disrupted. The <u>individual</u> is further <u>depersonalized</u> by

Personality altered

the issuance of a uniform, confiscation of belongings, and gathering of personal information, as well as by more subtle touches like doorless toilets, record keeping, and bedchecks. The effects of an institutional setting are so all-encompassing that one can meaningfully speak of an "institutional personality": a persistent manner of behaving compliantly and without emotional involvement.

Becomes psychotic, childlike, or depressive

Of course, there are individual differences in adaptation to the situation. They can be as extreme as psychosis, childlike regression, and depression or as mild as resigned compliance. Most individuals do adjust and build up a system of satisfactions, such as close friendships and cliques.

Individuals adjust but have trouble later on street

But because of these bonds and the fact that the habits needed to function in the outside world have been lost, inmates face great problems upon leaving an institution. A shift from the top of a small society to the bottom of a larger one may be further demoralizing.

Outlining

After reading, underlining, and annotating the piece, the next step could be to outline it. If the piece is well organized, you should be able to reduce it to a simple outline so that you can, at a glance, see the relationship of ideas (sequence, relative importance, and interdependence).

The essay on total institutions can be outlined very easily:

Total Institutions
  I. Common characteristics
     A. All activities in the same setting
     B. All phases of life within larger group
     C. Activities scheduled according to a master plan
        1. Bureaucratic society
        2. Social distance between inmates and staff
 II. Adjusting to the world inside
     A. Individual depersonalized
        1. Wears uniform
        2. No personal belongings
        3. No privacy
     B. Adaptation

1. Negative
   a. Psychosis
   b. Regression
   c. Depression
2. Positive

III. Problems upon release outside
   A. Adjusting to a different system
   B. Encountering shock of going to the bottom of a new order

Exercise 1 Underlining, Annotating, and Outlining

Underline and annotate the following passage. Then complete the outline that follows.

Effective E-Mail Practices

Scot Ober

1   Use short lines and short paragraphs. A short line length (perhaps 50 to 60 characters) is much easier to read than the 80-character line of most text editors. Similarly, short paragraphs (especially the first and last paragraphs) are more inviting to read. Avoid formatting a long message as one solid paragraph.

2   Don't shout. Use all-capital letters only for emphasis or to substitute for italicized text (such as book titles). Do NOT type your entire message in all capitals: It is a text-based form of *shouting* at your reader and is considered rude (not to mention being more difficult to read).

3   Proofread your message before sending it. Don't let the speed and convenience of e-mail lull you into being careless. While an occasional typo or other surface error will probably be overlooked by the reader, excessive errors or sloppy language creates an unprofessional image of the sender.

4   Append previous messages appropriately. Most e-mail systems allow you to append the original message to your reply. Use this feature judiciously. Occasionally, it may be helpful for the reader to see his or her entire message replayed. More often, however, you can save the reader time by establishing the context of the original message in your reply. If necessary, quote

pertinent parts of the original message. If the entire original message is needed, treat it as an appendix and insert it at the *end* of your reply—not at the beginning.

5   Use a direct style of writing and think twice; write once. Put your major idea in the first sentence or two. If the message is so sensitive or emotionally laden that a more indirect organization would be appropriate, you should reconsider whether e-mail is the most effective medium for the message. Because it is so easy to respond immediately to a message, you might be tempted to let your emotions take over. Such behavior is called "flaming" and should be avoided. Always assume the message you send will never be destroyed but will be saved permanently in somebody's computer file.

6   Don't neglect your greeting and closing. Downplay the seeming impersonality of computerized mail by starting your message with a friendly salutation, such as "Hi, Amos" or "Dear Mr. Fisher."

7   An effective closing is equally important. Some e-mail programs identify only the e-mail address (for example, "70511.753@compuserve.com") in the message header they transmit. Don't take a chance that your reader won't recognize you. Include your name, e-mail address, and any other appropriate identifying information at the end of your message.

—Adapted from *Contemporary Business Communication*

I. Short lines; short paragraphs

A. _____

B. _____

II. No shouting

A. No entire message in capital letters

B. Causes problems

1. _____

2. _____

III. Proofread message before sending

    A. Resist temptation to send without checking

    B. Errors create unprofessional image

IV. Append messages appropriately

    A. _____

    B. Often better to establish context in your message

    C. _____

V. Direct style with deliberation

    A. _____

    B. _____

VI. Greetings and closings

    A. _____

    B. Provide necessary information in closing

       1. _____

       2. _____

       3. _____

✳ Types of Reading-Related Writing

Many college writing tasks will require you to evaluate and reflect on what you read. You will be expected to read, think, and write. Your reading-related writing assignment may call for

- a **summary** (main ideas in your own words)
- a **reaction** (usually ideas on how the reading relates specifically to you, your experiences, and your attitudes but also often a critique of the worth and logic of the reading)

- a **two-part response** (includes both a summary and a reaction but separates them)

These kinds of writing have certain points in common. They originate as a response to something you have read and they indicate, to some degree, the content of the piece.

Writing a Summary

A **summary** is a rewritten, shortened version of a piece of writing in which you use your own wording to express the main ideas. Learning to summarize effectively will help you in many ways. Summary writing reinforces comprehension skills in reading. It requires you to discriminate among the ideas in the target reading passage. Summaries are usually written in the form of a well-designed paragraph or paragraph unit. Frequently, they are used in collecting material for research papers and in writing conclusions to essays.

The following rules will guide you in writing effective summaries. A summary

1. cites the author and title of the text.
2. is usually shorter than the original by about two-thirds, although the exact reduction will vary depending on the content of the original.
3. concentrates on the main ideas and includes details only infrequently.
4. changes the original wording without changing the idea.
5. does not evaluate the content or give an opinion in any way (even if you see an error in logic or fact).
6. does not add ideas (even if you have an abundance of related information).
7. does not include any personal comments by the author of the summary (therefore, no use of *I* referring to self).
8. seldom contains quotations (but if you do use quotations, do so only with quotation marks).
9. uses some author tags ("says York," "according to York," or "the author explains") to remind readers that the material is a summary of the material of another author.

Exercise 2   Evaluating a Summary

Apply the rules of summary writing to the following summary of "Total Institutions," pages 3–4. Mark the instances of poor summary writing by using rule numbers from the preceding list.

Total Institutions

A total institution completely encompasses the individual. Total institutions have certain common characteristics. Institutions provide the setting for all rest, recreation, and labor. Residents function only within the group. And residents are directed by a highly organized schedule, which, I think, is what they need or they wouldn't be there. There, residents are depersonalized by being required to wear a uniform, abandon personal items, and give up privacy. Some adapt in a negative way by developing psychological problems, but most adapt in a positive way by forming relationships with other residents. Several popular movies, such as *The Shawshank Redemption,* show how prison society works, to use one example. Once outside the total institution, individuals must deal with the problem of relearning old coping habits. They must also withstand the shock of going from the top of a small society to the bottom of a larger one. Society needs these total institutions, especially the jails.

The following is an example of an effective summary of "Total Institutions."

A Summary of "Total Institutions"
Michael Balleau

In "Total Institutions" Seymour Feshbach
and Bernard Weiner explain that a total
institution encompasses the lives of its
residents, who share three common traits: The
residents must do everything in the same
place, must do things together, and must do
things according to the institution's
schedule. The institution takes away the
residents' roles they had in society, takes
away their appearance by issuing uniforms,
takes away their personal property by
confiscation, and takes away their privacy by
making life communal. The authors say that
some residents adapt negatively by having
psychological problems, but most form
relationships and new roles within the
institution. Upon release, these residents
must learn to function in the free world all
over again as they start at the bottom of
society. This shift "may be further
demoralizing."

Writing a Reaction

The reaction statement is another kind of reading-related writing.
Some reactions require evaluation with a critical-thinking emphasis. Some focus on simple discussion of the content presented in the
reading and include summary material. Others concentrate on the
writer's experiences as related to the content of the passage.

The following paragraph is a student's reaction statement to "Total Institutions."

Institutions Always Win

Tanya Morris

The short essay "Total Institutions," by Seymour Feshbach and Bernard Weiner, is a study of conflicts in different settings. The common characteristics of such an institution are in personal combat with the individual, in which the resident is stripped of his or her choices and left to participate in all activities in the same setting, with no opportunity for a sanctuary. Further, the resident who tries to assert his or her uniqueness is controlled by a master plan. That plan is enforced by police personnel, who become the masters, set up social barriers, and maintain control over their underlings. Cut off from the free world, the resident is in conflict with significant matters of newness--clothes, facilities, regulations, and roles. The authors explain that inexorably the institution wins, converting the resident into a disturbed person or an amiable robot among others who are similarly institutionalized. But at that moment of conversion, the now-depersonalized individual may be thrust back into society to

try to reclaim old roles and behaviors in
another cycle of conflicts. The authors of
this essay are very clear in showing just how
comprehensive these institutions are in
waging their war, for good or bad, against
individuality. After all, they are "total."

Writing a Two-Part Response

As you have seen, the reaction response includes a partial summary
or is written with the assumption that readers have read the original piece. However, your instructor may prefer that you separate
each form—for example, by presenting a clear, concise summary
followed by a reaction response. This format is especially useful for
critical examination of a text or for problem-solving assignments,
because it requires you to understand and repeat another's views or
experiences before responding. The two-part approach also helps
you avoid the common problem of writing only a summary of the
text when your instructor wants you to both summarize and evaluate or otherwise react. In writing a summary and a reaction, it is a
good idea to ask your instructor if you should separate your summary from your response.

Total Institutions: A Summary and a Reaction

Michael Balleau

Summary

In "Total Institutions" Seymour Feshbach
and Bernard Weiner explain that a total
institution encompasses the lives of its
residents, who share three common traits: The
residents must do everything in the same
place, must do things together, and must do
things according to the institution's
schedule. The institution takes away the
residents' roles they had in society, takes

away their appearance by issuing uniforms,
takes away their personal property by
confiscation, and takes away their privacy by
making life communal. The authors say that
some residents adapt negatively by having
psychological problems, but most form
relationships and new roles within the
institution. Upon release, these residents
must learn to function in the free world all
over again as they start at the bottom of
society. This shift "may be further
demoralizing."

Reaction

The basic ideas in "Total Institutions"
gave me an insight into the behavior of my
cousin. Let's call him George. He spent almost
five years in prison for white collar crime at
the bank where he worked. When George was
incarcerated, he was an individual, almost to
the extreme of being a rebel. When he got out,
he was clearly an institutionalized person.
Cut off from the consumer society, George was
reluctant to enter stores and go through
checkout lines. He was fearful of being left
alone. Because his prison setting was very
noisy, silence made him uncomfortable, and he
wanted a radio or television on all the time.

> Accustomed to being around people in the
> institution, George couldn't stand being
> alone, and he depended on others to suggest
> times for meals and chores. Of course, his new
> reputation and behavior now set him apart from
> his former roles. It took him almost three
> years to readjust.

Exercise 3   Suggestions for Reading-Related Writing

Complete one of the following reading-related responses.

1. Write a summary of "Effective E-Mail Practices" on pages 5–6.

2. Write a two-part response composed of labeled summary and reaction parts based on "Effective E-Mail Practices."

✳ Writer's Guidelines at a Glance: Reading Effectively and Writing Summaries

1. **Underlining** helps you to read with discrimination.

   - Underline the main ideas in paragraphs.
   - Underline the support for those ideas.
   - Underline answers to questions that you bring to the reading assignment.
   - Underline only the key words.

2. **Annotating** enables you to actively engage the reading material.

   - Number parts if appropriate.
   - Make comments according to your interests and needs.

3. **Outlining** the passages you read sheds light on the relationship of ideas, including the major divisions of the passage and their relative importance.

4. **Summarizing** helps you concentrate on main ideas. A summary

   - cites the author and title of the text.
   - is usually shorter than the original by about two-thirds, although the exact reduction will vary depending on the content of the original.
   - concentrates on the main ideas and includes details only infrequently.
   - changes the original wording without changing the idea.
   - does not evaluate the content or give an opinion in any way (even if you see an error in logic or fact).
   - does not add ideas (even if you have an abundance of related information).
   - does not include any personal comments by the author of the summary (therefore, no use of *I* referring to self).
   - seldom uses quotations (but if you do use quotations, do so only with quotation marks).
   - uses some author tags ("says York," "according to York," or "the author explains") to remind readers that the material is a summary of the material of another writer.

5. **Writing a reaction** (an explanation of how the reading relates to you, your experiences, and your attitudes; also, often your critique of the worth and logic of the piece) or a *two-part response* (a separate summary and reaction) allows you to examine written material.

✳ 2

The Paragraph and Prewriting

✳ The Paragraph Defined

Paragraphs for written assignments are easy to spot because they are indented: Each one starts with skipped spaces at the beginning of the first line. The kind of paragraph we will consider in this book contains three parts: the subject, the topic sentence, and the support.

The **subject** is what you will write about. That subject is likely to be broad and must be focused for more specific treatment. The **topic sentence** includes both the subject and the specific treatment of that subject. The treatment tells what you plan to *do* with the subject.

The topic sentence contains the central, or main, idea of the paragraph. Everything else in the paragraph supports the topic sentence; that is, all the other sentences explain or say more about the central idea. The **support** is the evidence or reasoning that explains the topic sentence. That support can be developed according to several basic patterns. Each pattern is the subject of one chapter of this book. The following questions can help you choose an appropriate pattern or a combination of patterns for your paragraph.

Narration: Can you illustrate your point by telling a story?

Description: How does something look, sound, feel, taste, or smell?

Exemplification: Can you support your main idea with examples of what you mean?

Analysis by division: What are the parts of a unit, and how do they work together?

Process analysis: How do you do something? How is (was) something done?

Cause and effect: What are the reasons for or the results of an event, a trend, or a circumstance?

Classification: How can the ideas, persons, or things be grouped?

Comparison and contrast: How are two or more subjects similar and different?

16

Definition: What does a term mean?
Argument: What evidence and reasoning will convince someone that you are right?

These patterns are often combined in writing. Regardless of the pattern or combination you use, the structure of the paragraph remains the same. A **paragraph** is a group of sentences, each with the function of supporting a single main idea, which is contained in the topic sentence. Here is a good example:

> A cat's tail is a good barometer of its intentions. An excited or aggressively aroused cat will whip its entire tail back and forth. When I talk to Sam, he holds up his end of the conversation by occasionally flicking the tip of his tail. Mother cats move their tails back and forth to invite their kittens to play. A kitten raises its tail perpendicularly to beg for attention; older cats may do so to beg for food. When your cat holds its tail aloft while crisscrossing in front of you, it is trying to say, "Follow me"—usually to the kitchen, or more precisely, to the refrigerator. Unfortunately, many cats have lost their tails in refrigerator doors as a consequence.

> *–Michael W. Fox,* "What Is Your Pet Trying to Tell You?"

The paragraph begins with the topic sentence: "A cat's tail is a good barometer of its intentions." The other sentences provide support for the topic sentence; they give examples to show that the topic sentence is true. The final sentence adds humor to the writing and gives a sense of ending, or closure.

Although the topic sentence is often the first sentence of the paragraph, it does not have to be. Furthermore, the topic sentence is sometimes restated or echoed at the end of the paragraph, although again it does not have to be. However, a well-phrased concluding sentence can emphasize the central idea of the paragraph as well as provide a nice balance and ending.

A paragraph is not a constraining formula; in fact, it has variations. In some instances, for example, the topic sentence is not found in a single sentence. It may be the combination of two sentences, or it may be an easily understood but unwritten underlying idea that unifies the paragraph. Nevertheless, the paragraph in most college writing contains discussion that supports a stated topic sentence, and the instruction in this book is based on that fundamental idea.

✳ A Sample Paragraph

The following paragraph was written by college student Cyrus Norton. The subject of the paragraph and the treatment of the paragraph have been underlined. Norton's topic sentence (not the first sentence in this case), his support of the topic sentence, and his concluding sentence have been identified in the margin.

This is the final draft. Following it, we will back up and, in this chapter and the next, show how Norton moved during the writing process from his initial idea to this polished paragraph.

Magic Johnson, an NBA Great

Cyrus Norton

Some NBA (National Basketball Association) players are good because they have a special talent in one area. **Magic Johnson was a great NBA star because he was excellent in shooting, passing, rebounding, and leading.** As a shooter, few have ever equaled him. He could slam, shovel, hook, and fire from three-point range--all with deadly accuracy. As for free throws, he led all NBA players in shooting percentage in 1988-89. While averaging more than twenty points per game, he helped others become stars with his passes. As the point guard (the quarterback of basketball), he was always near the top in the league in assists and was famous for his "no-look" pass, which often surprised even his teammates with its precision. When he

Margin annotations:

Topic sentence

Support for shooting

Support for passing

wasn't shooting or passing, he was

Support for rebounding rebounding. A top rebounding guard is unusual in professional basketball, but Magic, at six feet, nine inches, could bump shoulders and leap with anyone. These three qualities made him probably the most spectacular triple-double threat of all time. "Triple-double" means reaching two digits in scoring, assists, and rebounding. Magic didn't need more for greatness in the NBA, but he had more. With his everlasting smile and

Support for leading boundless energy, he was also an inspirational team leader. He always believed in himself and his team. When his team was down by a point and three seconds remained on the game clock, the fans looked for Magic to get the ball. They watched as he dribbled once, he faded, he leaped, he twisted, and he hooked one in from twenty feet! That was

Concluding sentence magic. That was Magic.

Let's consider Norton's paragraph in the light of what we know about paragraphs in general. Magic Johnson, the subject, is what the paragraph is all about. In this example, the title also names the subject. The topic sentence, the unifying and controlling idea, makes a clear statement about what the writer will say about the subject. As usual, the topic sentence appears near the beginning of the paragraph. The support gives evidence and examples to back up the controlling idea. The last sentence, "That was Magic," echoes the topic sentence. It is usually called the concluding sentence.

The author has told you what he was going to say, he has said it, and finally he has reminded you of what he has told you.

The concluding sentence is sometimes omitted. The two most common designs of paragraphs in college writing are these:

Topic sentence→support→concluding sentence
Topic sentence→support

"Magic Johnson, an NBA Great" is a typical paragraph: a group of sentences that present and develop an idea. In college writing a paragraph is usually expository; that is, its purpose is to explain. In this example, you, the reader, get the point. You're informed, and maybe even entertained a little by the explanation.

If you follow certain principles and then practice, practice, practice, you too can write effective paragraphs. Success lies in following directions and using the right set of tools.

Principles at a Glance

Paragraph:	A group of sentences that present and develop an idea.
Topic sentence:	The sentence that expresses the controlling idea of the paragraph. The topic sentence mentions the subject (what the paragraph is about) and the treatment (what the writer will say about the subject).
Support:	Evidence such as details, examples, and explanations that explain the topic sentence.
Basic paragraph designs:	Topic sentence→support→concluding sentence Topic sentence→support

---

☀ The Writing Process

There are easy, comfortable, and effective ways to write a paragraph. Writing does not mean merely putting words on paper. It is a process that often involves several steps: using prewriting techniques to explore a topic, limiting and then developing the topic, making an outline, writing a draft, revising the draft as many times as necessary, and editing. Writers sometimes discover that their topic sentence or their outline does not work, and they go back and alter their original concept or design.

For flexible, systematic guidance, consider the Writing Process Worksheet on page xx. It can be copied, enlarged, and submitted with your assignment, if your instructor asks you to do so.

✳ Prewriting: Using the Blank Sheet of Opportunity

Certain strategies commonly grouped under the heading *prewriting* can help you get started and develop your ideas. Actually, these strategies—freewriting, brainstorming, clustering, defining a topic, and outlining—are very much a part of writing. The understandable desire to skip to the finished statement is what causes the most common student-writer grief: that of not filling the blank sheet or of filling it but not significantly improving on the blankness. The prewriting strategies that follow will help you attack the blank sheet constructively with imaginative thought, analysis, and experimentation. They can lead to clear, effective communication.

Although the strategies can work very well, you do not need to use all of them in all writing assignments. Learn them now, and use them when they are needed. Think of this approach as carrying a box of tools and then selecting the best tools for the job.

Freewriting

Freewriting is an exercise that its originator, Peter Elbow, has called "babbling in print." In freewriting, you write without stopping, letting your ideas tumble forth. You do not concern yourself with the fundamentals of writing, such as punctuation and spelling. Freewriting is an adventure into your memory and imagination. It is concerned with discovery, invention, and exploration. If you are at a loss for words on your subject, write in a comment such as "I don't know what is coming next" or "blah, blah, blah," and continue when relevant words come. The important thing is to not stop writing. Freewriting immediately eliminates the blank page and thereby helps you break through an emotional barrier, but that is not the only benefit. The words that you sort through in that idea kit will include some you can use. You can then underline or circle those words, and even add notes on the side so that the freewriting continues to grow even after its initial spontaneous expression.

The way in which you proceed depends on the type of assignment:

working with a topic of your choice,
working from a restricted list of topics, or
working with a prescribed topic.

The *topic of your choice* affords you the greatest freedom of exploration. You would probably select a subject that interests you and freewrite about it, allowing your mind to wander among its many parts, perhaps mixing fact and fantasy, direct experience, and hearsay. A freewriting about music might uncover areas of special interest and knowledge, such as jazz or folk rock, that you would want to pursue further in freewriting or other prewriting strategies.

Working from a *restricted list* requires a more focused freewriting. With the list, you can, of course, experiment with several topics to discover what is most suitable for you. If, for example, "career choice," "career preparation," "career guidance," and "career prospects" are on the restricted list, you would probably select one and freewrite about it. If it works well for you, you would probably proceed with the next step of your prewriting. If you are not satisfied with what you uncover in freewriting, you would explore another item from the restricted list.

When working with a *prescribed topic,* you focus on a particular topic and try to restrict your freewriting to its boundaries. If your topic specifies a division of a subject area such as "political involvement of your generation," then you would tie those key words to your own information, critical thinking, and imaginative responses. If the topic is restricted to, let's say, your reaction to a particular reading selection such as a poem, then that poem would give you the framework for your free associations with your own experiences, creations, and opinions.

You should learn to use freewriting because it will often serve you well, but you need not use it every time you write. Some very short writing assignments do not call for freewriting. An in-class assignment may not allow time for freewriting.

Nevertheless, freewriting is often a useful strategy in your toolbox of writing techniques. It can help you get words on paper, break emotional barriers, generate topics, develop new insights, and explore ideas.

Freewriting can lead to other stages of prewriting and writing, and it can also provide content as you develop your topic.

The following example of freewriting, and the writing, revising, and editing examples in Chapter 3, are from student Cyrus Norton's paragraph, "Magic Johnson, an NBA Great" (pp. 18–19). Norton's topic came from a restricted list; he was directed to write about the success of an individual. Had he been working with a prescribed topic, he might have been directed to concentrate on a specific aspect of Johnson's career, such as business, philanthropy, public service, or the one Norton chose: great basketball playing.

Sample Freewriting

great   Magic Johnson was the <u>greatest</u> player I've ever seen in professional basketball.

leader   Actually not just a player but a <u>leader</u> and **inspiration**   an <u>inspiration</u> to the team so they always gave him the ball when the game was on the line. It was too bad his career was cut short when they discovered he was HIV positive. Actually he came back but then retired again.

rich   He made <u>a lot of money</u> and I guess he invested it wisely because his name is linked to the Lakers and theaters and more. Also to programs making people aware of the danger of AIDS and helping kids grow up and stay out of trouble. But the main thing about Magic is **playing**   the <u>way he played</u>. He could do everything. He even played center one time in a championship **scoring**   game. He always <u>scored a lot</u> and he could **passing**   <u>pass</u> like nobody else. Even though he was a **rebounding**   guard, he was tall and could <u>rebound</u>. He was great. Everyone says so.

After doing this freewriting, Cyrus Norton went back through his work looking for ideas that might be developed in a paper.

Observe how he returned to his freewriting and examined it for possible ideas to develop for a writing assignment. As he recognized those ideas, he underlined key words and phrases and made a few notes in the margins. By reading only the underlined words, you can obtain a basic understanding of what is important to him. It is not necessary to underline entire sentences.

In addition to putting some words on that dreaded blank sheet of paper, Norton discovered that he had quite a lot of information about Magic Johnson and that he had selected a favorable topic to develop. The entire process took little time. Had he found few or no promising ideas, he might have freewritten about another topic. In going back through his work, he saw some errors in writing, but he did not correct them because the purpose of freewriting is discovery, not correct grammar, punctuation, or spelling. He was confident that he could then continue with the process of writing a paper.

Brainstorming

Brainstorming features key words and phrases that relate in various ways to the subject area or to the specific topic you are concerned with. One effective way to get started is to ask the big-six questions about your subject area: *Who? What? Where? When? Why?* and *How?* Then let your mind run free as you jot down answers in single entries or lists. Some of the big-six questions may not fit, and some may be more important than others, depending on the purposes of your writing. For example, if you were writing about the causes of a situation, the *Why?* question could be more important than the others; if you were concerned with how to do something, the *How?* question would predominate. If you were writing in response to a reading selection, you would confine your thinking to questions appropriately related to the content of that reading selection.

Whatever your focus for the questions is, the result is likely to be numerous ideas that will provide information for continued exploration and development of your topic. Thus your pool of information for writing widens and deepens.

An alternative to the big-six-questions approach is simply to make a list of words and phrases related to your subject area or specific topic.

Cyrus Norton continued with the topic of Magic Johnson, and his topic tightened to focus on particular areas. Although Norton could have listed the annotations and the words he underlined in his freewriting, he used the big-six questions for his framework.

Who?   Magic Johnson
What?   great basketball player
Where?   the NBA
When?   for more than ten years
Why?   love of game and great talent
How?   shooting, passing, rebounding, leading, coolness, inspiring

As it turned out, *How?* was the most fruitful question for Norton, and it led him to a list.

Clustering

Clustering (also called **mapping**) is yet another prewriting technique. Start by double-bubbling your topic; that is, write it down in the middle of the page and draw a double circle around it. Then respond

to the question "What comes to mind?" Single-bubble other ideas on spokes radiating out from the hub that contains the topic. Any bubble can lead to another bubble or numerous bubbles in the same way. This strategy is sometimes used instead of or before making an outline to organize and develop ideas.

The more specific the topic inside the double bubble, the fewer the number of spokes that will radiate with single bubbles. For example, a topic such as "high school dropouts" would have more spokes than "reasons for dropping out of high school."

See Cyrus Norton's cluster (on the preceding page) on the subject of Magic Johnson.

✳ Writing the Topic Sentence

The topic sentence is the most important sentence in your prewriting and also in your paragraph. It includes two parts: the subject and the treatment, what you will do with your subject. Consider, for example, this topic sentence:

<u>Magic Johnson</u> <u>was a great all-around NBA player.</u>
    subject   treatment

It is an effective topic sentence because it limits the subject and indicates treatment that can be developed in additional sentences. Another sound version is the following, which goes further to include divisions for the treatment.

<u>Magic Johnson</u> <u>was a great NBA star because he was excellent</u>
    subject   treatment
<u>in shooting, passing, rebounding, and leading.</u>

Ineffective topic sentences are often too broad, vague, or too narrow.

TOO BROAD OR VAGUE	Magic Johnson was everything to everybody.
	Magic Johnson was fun.
	Magic Johnson was a success in basketball.
TOO NARROW	Magic Johnson went to Michigan State University.
	Magic Johnson signed with the Los Angeles Lakers.

Usually, simple statements of fact do not need or do not allow for development.

Exercise 1 Evaluating Topic Sentences

Mark the following statements for subject (S) and treatment (T), and label each as effective (E) or ineffective (I). Effective statements are those that you can easily relate to supporting evidence. Ineffective statements are too broad, vague, or too narrow.

_____ 1. Columbus is located in Ohio.

_____ 2. Columbus is a fabulous city.

_____ 3. Columbus has dealt thoroughly with its housing problems.

_____ 4. A monkey is a primate.

_____ 5. Monkeys are fun.

_____ 6. In clinical studies, monkeys have demonstrated a remarkable ability to reason.

_____ 7. More than a million cats are born in California each year.

_____ 8. A simple observation of a domesticated cat in the pursuit of game will show that it has not lost its instinct for survival.

_____ 9. The two teams in the Rose Bowl have similar records.

_____ 10. Michigan State is in the Rose Bowl.

Exercise 2 Writing Topic Sentences

Complete the following entries by making each into a solid topic sentence. Only a subject and part of the treatment are provided. The missing part may be more than a single word.

EXAMPLE Car salespersons behave differently depending on <u>the car they are selling and the kind of customer they are serving.</u>

1. Television commercials are often _____

_____

2. Rap music promotes _____

_____

3. My part-time job taught me _____

_____

4. I promote environmental conservation by _____

_____

5. The clothing that a person wears often reveals _____

_____

6. My close friend is preoccupied with _____

_____

7. Winning a lot of money is not always _____

_____

8. Country music appeals to our most basic _____

_____

9. Friendship depends on _____

_____

10. A good salesperson should _____

_____

Exercise 3   Writing Topic Sentences

Write a topic sentence for each of the following subjects.

1. Computer literacy _____

_____

_____

2. My taste in music_____

_____

_____

3. Bus transportation _____

_____

_____

4. The fear of crime _____

_____

_____

5. An excellent boss _____

_____

_____

6. Doing well in college English classes _____

_____

_____

7. Violence on television_____

_____

_____

8. Child care centers_____

_____

_____

9. Good health _____

_____

_____

10. Teenage voters_____

_____

_____

✳ Writing the Outline

An **outline** is a pattern for showing the relationship of ideas. The two main outline forms are the **sentence outline** (each entry is a complete sentence) and the **topic outline** (each entry is a key word or phrase). The topic outline is commonly used for paragraphs.

Indentation, number and letter sequences, punctuation, and the placement of words are important to clear communication in an outline. We do not read an outline expecting to be surprised by form and content, as we do a poem. We go to the outline for information, and we expect to find ideas easily. Unconventional marks (circles, squares, half-parentheses) and items out of order are distracting and, therefore, undesirable in an outline. The standard form is as easily mastered as a nonstandard form, and it is worth your time to learn it. Outlining is not difficult: the pattern is flexible and can have any number of levels and parts.

Basically, an outline shows how a topic sentence is supported. Thus it shows the organization of the paragraph. The most important supporting material, called the **major support,** is indicated by Roman numerals. That major support is developed by less important supporting material, called the **minor support,** which in turn may be developed by details or examples. Here is the outline developed by Cyrus Norton:

Topic sentence   Magic Johnson was a great NBA star because he was excellent in shooting, passing, rebounding, and leading.

I. Shooting (major support)
   A. Short shots (minor support)
      1. Shovel (detail)
      2. Slam-dunk (detail)
   B. Long shots (minor support)
   C. Free throws (minor support)
II. Passing (major support)
   A. No-look (minor support)
   B. Precise (minor support)
III. Rebounding (major support)
   A. Leaping (minor support)
   B. Bumping shoulders (minor support)
IV. Leading (major support)
   A. Energy (minor support)
   B. Spirit (minor support)
      1. Faith (detail)
      2. Smile (detail)

The foundation of a good outline and hence a good paragraph is a strong topic sentence, which means one with a specific subject and a well-defined treatment. After writing a good topic sentence, the next step is to divide the treatment into parts. Just what the parts are will depend on what you are trying to do in the treatment. Consider the thought process involved. What sections of material would be appropriate in your discussion to support or explain that topic sentence?

Among the most common forms of division are the following:

- Divisions of time or incident to tell a story

  I. Situation
  II. Conflict
  III. Struggle
  IV. Outcome
  V. Meaning

- Divisions of examples or divisions of one example into three or more aspects

  I. First example (aspect)
  II. Second example (aspect)
  III. Third example (aspect)

- Divisions of causes or effects

  I. Cause (or effect) one
  II. Cause (or effect) two
  III. Cause (or effect) three

- Divisions of a unit into parts (such as the federal government into executive, legislative, and judicial branches—or Magic Johnson's all-around skill into shooting, passing, rebounding, and leading)

  I. Part one
  II. Part two
  III. Part three

- Divisions of how to do something or how something was done

  I. Preparation
  II. Steps
      A. Step 1
      B. Step 2
      C. Step 3

Exercise 4 Completing Basic Outline Patterns

Fill in the missing outline parts. Consider whether you are dealing with time, examples, causes, effects, parts, or steps. Answers will vary, depending on individual experiences and views.

1. Too many of us are preoccupied with material things.

    I. Clothing

    II. Cars

    III. _____

2. Television sitcoms may vary, but every successful show has certain components.

    I. Good acting

    II. _____

    III. Good situations

    IV. _____

3. A female who is trying to discourage unwanted sexual advances should take several measures.

    I. _____

    II. Set clear boundaries

    III. Avoid compromising situations

4. Concentrating during reading involves various techniques.

    I. Preview material

    II. Pose questions

    III. _____

5. Crime has some bad effects on a nearby neighborhood.

    I. People fearful

       A. Don't go out at night

       B. _____

    II. People without love for neighborhood

       A. _____

       B. Put houses up for sale

    III. People as victims

       A. Loss of possessions

       B. _____

6. Exercising can improve a person's life.

  I. Looks better

    A. Skin

    B. _____

  II. Feels better

    A. _____

    B. Body

  III. Performs better

    A. Work

    B. _____

7. Shoppers in department stores can be grouped according to needs.

  I. _____

  II. Special-needs shoppers

  III. Bargain hunters

8. There are different kinds of intelligence based on situations.

  I. Street-smart

  II. Common sense

  III. _____

9. Smoking should be discouraged.

  I. Harm to smokers

    A. _____

    B. Cancer risk

  II. Harm to those around smokers

    A. _____

    B. Fellow workers

  III. Cost

    A. Industry—production and absenteeism

    B. _____

10. An excellent police officer must have six qualities.

    I. _____

   II. Knowledge of law

  III. _____

  IV. Emotional soundness

   V. Skill in using weapons

 VI. _____

✳ Writer's Guidelines at a Glance: The Paragraph and Prewriting

1. A **paragraph** is a group of sentences, each with the function of stating or supporting a single controlling idea that is contained in the topic sentence.

2. A paragraph contains two parts: the topic sentence and the support.

   - The **topic sentence** expresses the controlling idea of the paragraph. It has a **subject** (what the paragraph is about) and a **treatment** (what the writer will do with the subject).
   - The **support** is the evidence, such as details, examples, and explanations, that backs up the topic sentence.

3. The two most common paragraph designs in college writing are these:

   - Topic sentence→support→concluding sentence
   - Topic sentence→support

4. Prewriting includes activities you do before writing your first draft or whenever you need new ideas.

   - **Freewriting:** writing without stopping, letting your ideas tumble forth. Freewriting helps you break emotional barriers, generate topics, and discover and explore ideas.
   - **Brainstorming:** a listing procedure that helps you discover key words and phrases that relate to your topic. Simply make a list, or ask *Who? What? Where? When? Why?* and *How?* questions of your topic.

- **Clustering:** a graphic way of showing connections and relationships. Start by double-bubbling your topic. Then ask "What comes to mind?" and single-bubble other ideas on spokes radiating out from the double bubble.
- **Writing the topic sentence:** the subject (what you are writing about) and treatment (what you are doing with your subject).
- **Writing the outline:** a form for indicating the relationship of ideas. An outline shows how a topic sentence is supported. Thus it reveals the organization of the paragraph. Major support is indicated by Roman numerals. The major support is developed by minor support, which in turn may be developed by details or examples.

Topic sentence
  I. Major support
    A. Minor support
    B. Minor support
      1. Details or examples
      2. Details or examples
 II. Major support
    A. Minor support
    B. Minor support

Writing, Revising, and Editing the Paragraph

✳ Writing Your First Draft

Once you have completed your topic sentence and outline (or list or cluster), you are ready to begin writing your paragraph. The initial writing is called the **first,** or **rough, draft.** Your topic sentence is likely to be at or near the beginning of your paragraph and will be followed by your support as ordered by your outline.

Paying close attention to your outline for basic organization, you should proceed without worrying about the refinements of writing. This is not the time to concern yourself with perfect spelling, grammar, or punctuation. After you have finished that first draft, take a close look at it. If your topic sentence is sound and your outline has served you well, you have a basic discussion. You have made a statement and supported it.

Don't be embarrassed by the roughness of your work. You should be embarrassed only if you leave it that way. You are seeing the reason why a first draft is called "rough." Famous authors have said publicly that they wouldn't show their rough drafts even to their closest, most forgiving friends.

The Recursive Factor

The process of writing can be called **recursive,** which means "going back and forth." In this respect, writing is like reading. If you do not understand what you have read, you back up and read it again. After you have reread a passage, you may still need to read selectively. The same can be said of writing. If, for example, after having developed an outline and started writing your first draft, you discover that your subject is too broad, you have to back up, narrow your topic sentence, and then adjust your outline. You may even want to return to an early cluster of ideas to see how you can use a smaller grouping of them. Revision is usually the most recursive of all parts of the writing process. You will go over your material again and again until you are satisfied that you have expressed yourself as well as you possibly can.

✳ Revising Your Writing

The term *first draft* suggests quite accurately that there will be other drafts, or versions, of your writing. Only in the most dire situations, such as an in-class examination when you have time for only one draft, should you be satisfied with a single effort.

What you do beyond the first draft is revising and editing. Revision is concerned with organization, content, and language effectiveness. Editing involves a final correcting of mistakes in spelling, punctuation, and capitalization. In practice, editing and revision are not always separate activities, although writers usually wait until the next-to-the-last draft to edit some minor details and attend to other small points that can be easily overlooked.

Successful revision almost always involves intense, systematic rewriting. You should learn to look for certain aspects of skillful writing as you enrich and repair your first draft. To help you recall these aspects so that you can keep them in mind and examine your material comprehensively, this textbook offers a memory device—an acronym in which each letter suggests an important feature of good writing and revision. This device enables you to memorize the features of good writing quickly. Soon you will be able to recall and refer to them automatically. These features need not be attended to individually when you revise your writing, although they may be. And they need not be attended to in the order presented here. The acronym is CLUESS (pronounced "clues"), which provides this guide:

Coherence
Language
Unity
Emphasis
Support
Sentences

Coherence

Coherence is the flow of ideas, with each idea leading logically and smoothly to the next. It is achieved by numbering parts or otherwise indicating time (*first, second, third, then, next, soon,* and so on), giving directions (according to space, as in "To the right is a map, and to the left of that map is a bulletin board"), using transitional words (*however, otherwise, therefore, similarly, hence, on the other hand, then, consequently, accordingly, thus*), using demonstrative pronouns (*this, that, those*), and moving in a clear order (from the least important to the most important or from the most important to the least important).

Language

Language here means using words that are suitable for what you are writing and for your audience. In college writing that means you will usually avoid slang and clichés such as "a barrel of laughs," "happy as a clam," and "six of one and a half dozen of another." Your writing will contain standard grammar and usage. Effective writing also includes words that will convey your ideas with precision. Avoid general words such as "transportation" when a specific one such as "bus" would serve you better. Also avoid abstract words such as "cool" when a concrete word or phrase such as "faded jeans" would make your meaning clear.

Unity

Unity begins with a good topic sentence. Everything in your paragraph should be related and subordinated to your topic sentence. Repetition of a key word or phrase can make the unity even stronger.

Emphasis

Emphasize, or stress, important ideas by using **position** (the most emphatic parts of a work are the beginning and the end), **repetition** (repeat key words and phrases), and **isolation** (a short, direct sentence among longer ones will usually command attention).

Support

Support is the material that backs up, justifies, or proves your topic sentence. Work carefully with the material from your outline (or list or cluster) to make sure that your ideas are well supported. If your paragraph is skimpy and your ideas slender, you are probably generalizing and not explaining how you arrived at your conclusions. Avoid repetition that does not add to the content; use details and examples; indicate parts and discuss relationships; and explain why your generalizations are true, logical, and accurate. Your reader can't accept your ideas unless he or she knows by what reasoning or use of evidence you developed them.

Sentences

Be sure your **sentences** are complete (not fragments) and that you have not incorrectly combined word groups that should be sentences (comma splices and run-ons). Consider using different types of sentences and different sentence beginnings. (See Handbook, p. 172.)

Write as many drafts as necessary, revising as you go for all the aspects of effective writing. Don't confuse revising with editing (the final stage of the writing process); don't get bogged down in fixing such things as spelling and punctuation.

✳ Adding Editing to Your Revision

Editing, the final stage of the writing process, involves a careful examination of your work. Look for problems with *c*apitalization, *o*missions, *p*unctuation, and *s*pelling (COPS).

Before you submit your writing to your instructor, do what almost all professional writers do before sending their material along: Read it aloud, to yourself or to a willing accomplice. Reading material aloud will help you catch any awkwardness of expression, omission and misplacement of words, and other problems that are easily overlooked by an author.

As you can see, writing is a process and is not a matter of just sitting down and "banging out" a statement. The parts of the process from prewriting to revising to editing are connected, and your movement is ultimately forward, but this process allows you to go back and forth in the recursive manner discussed earlier. If your outline is not working, perhaps the flaw is in your topic sentence. You may need to go back and fix it. If one section of your paragraph is skimpy, perhaps you will have to go back and reconsider the pertinent material in your outline or cluster. There you might find more details or alter a statement so that you can move into more fertile areas of thought.

Cyrus Norton wrote this first draft, marked it for revision, and then completed the final draft, which you read on pages 18–19. For simplification, only this draft is shown, although a typical paper might require several drafts, including one on which the author has done nothing but edit his or her revised writing.

Magic Johnson ~~,~~ *an NBA Great*

(National Basketball Association)

Some NBA players are good because they

have a special talent

~~are good~~ in one area ~~such as shooting,~~

~~passing, or rebounding.~~ Magic Johnson was *a*

NBA star   *excellent*   *shooting, passing,*

great because he was ~~good~~ in ~~all of those~~

rebounding, and leading

~~things and more.~~ As a shooter few have ~~been~~

ever equaled him

~~able to do what he could.~~ He could slam,

shovel, hook, and fire from three-point

—all with deadly accuracy   *As for*

ran~~ge.~~ge. ~~When it came to~~ free throws, he led

all NBA players in shooting percentage in

While

1988-89. ~~Then~~ he averaged more than twenty

points per game, he helped others become

with his passes   *(the quarterback of basketball)*

stars. As the point guard he was always near

the top in the league in a*s*sists and was

famous for his "no-look" passes *w*hich often

its

surprised even his teammates with ~~their~~

When he wasn't shooting or passing, he was rebounding.

precision. A top rebounding guard is unusual,

but Magic, ~~standing~~ at six feet nine inches

u

tall, could bump sholders and jump with

anyone. These three qualities made him

probably the most spectacular triple-double

"Triple-double" means reaching two digits in scoring, assists, and rebounding.

threat of all time. Magic didn't need more
                           ∧

for greatness in the NBA, but he had more. He
                                              ∧

was also an inspirational team leader with
                                       ≡

his everlasting smile and boundless energy.
                                          ∧

He   ed
∧Always believing in himself and his team.
∧   ∧

When his team was down by a point and three

           remained on the game clock   *the fans*
seconds ~~were left~~, ~~you~~ always looked for
        ∧   ∧
                                         They
Magic to get the ball. ~~Then you~~ watched as he
                                     ∧

              he   he   he
dribbled once, faded, leaped, twisted, and
              ∧   ∧   ∧

he   *That was magic.*
∧hooked one in from twenty feet That was
∧   ∧∧

Magic.

Exercise 1 Revising and Editing

*Treat the following paragraph as your own rough draft, and mark
it in the way Cyrus Norton marked his rough draft. First consider
coherence, language, unity, emphasis, support, and sentences
(CLUESS). Then edit the paragraph, correcting fundamentals such
as capitalization, omissions, punctuation, and spelling (COPS).*

High school dress codes don't make any sense to me.
I've heard all the reasons. Too many kids wear gang
clothes and some get attacked or even killed. Parents
have to put up too much money and even then the kids
without parents with deep pockets can't compete. And then
there are those that say kids behave bad if they dress in
a free spirit way. Let's take them one at a time. As for
the gang stuff, it's mainly how you act, not how you

look, and if the gang stuff is still a problem, then just
ban certain items of clothing. You don't have to go to
the extreames of uniforms, just change the attitude, not
the clothes. Then comes the money angle. Let the kid get
a part-time job if they want better clothes. The behavior
number is not what I can relate to. I mean, you go to
class and learn, and you do it the school way, but the
way you dress should have something to do with how you
want to express yourself. Do they want to turn out a
bunch of little robots that think the same way, behave
the same way, and yes with the dress code even look the
same way. Get real! If they'll cut us some slack with how
we dress, they'll get happier campers in the classroom.
Later better-citizens in society.

Exercise 2 Revising and Editing

*Mark the following rough draft for **c**oherence, **l**anguage, **u**nity, em-*
*phasis, **s**upport, and **s**entences (CLUESS). Then edit it, correcting*
*fundamentals such as **c**apitalization, **o**missions, **p**unctuation, and*
spelling (COPS).

Some young voters are not voting the way they should.
The latest figures show that only twenty percent are
going to the poles. An older generation, the so-called
baby boomers, is going to the poles at about twice that
rate. Since I'm young, I'm concerned, but the answers to
why we usually don't bother to vote are as obvious as the
nose on your face. For one thing the younger people don't
think that voting changes anything. The political parties
are all about the same and the candidates look and talk

alike, even though they seem angry with each other. For another a lot of young voters don't have parents that voted or even talked about politics when they were growing up, they don't either. Still another thing is that the issues going around don't move young people that much. The politicians talk about the national debt and social security and health care and we're concerned about jobs and the high cost of education. If they could get people we could believe in and they would talk about issue that matter to us, then maybe they'd see more of us at the polls.

Exercise 3 Revising and Editing

Mark the following rough draft for coherence, language, unity, emphasis, support, and sentences (CLUESS). Then edit it, correcting fundamentals such as capitalization, omissions, punctuation, and spelling (COPS).

Make me a traffic cop, and I'll crack down on certain types of driver. First off are the drunks. I'd zap them off the highways right off, and any cop would. But what I'm really talking about is the jerks of the highway. Near the top are the up-tight lane changers, for example, this morning when I was driving to school, I saw several. I could have carved at least a couple notches in a vilation pad, and I wasn't even cranky. They cut off people and force their way in, and leave behind upset and hurt people. Then there's the left-turn bullies the ones that keep moving out when the yellow turn to red. They come in all ages and sexes, they can be young or old, male or female. Yesterday, I saw this female in a pick-up barrel right out into the teeth of a red light. She had a baby on board. She had lead in her foot. She had evil in her eye. She was hostile and self-centered. Taking advantage of others. She knew that the facing traffic would probably not pull out and risk a head-on crash. The key word there is probably but many times people with a green light do move out and colide with the left turn bullies. Third, I'd sap the tailgaters. No one goes fast enough for these guys. I'm not alone in this peeve. One bumper sticker reads, "Stay back. I chew tobacky." And James Bond sprayed oil on cars that chased him. Since the first is dirty and the second is against the law, if I had the clout of a Rambo-cop I'd just rack up a lot of tailgater tickets. But there's a lot of road demons out there. Maybe it's good I'm not a traffic cop, Rambo or otherwise, cause traffic cops are suppose to inforce hundreds of laws. I don't know if I'd have time cause I have my own pet peeves in mind.

Exercise 4   Writing a Paragraph

Fill in the following two blanks to complete the topic sentence.

_____ *[person's name] is an excellent* _____
[boss, coach, doctor, neighbor, parent, preacher, teacher, sibling].

Then use the topic sentence to write a paragraph. Go through the complete writing process. Use one or more prewriting techniques (freewriting, brainstorming, clustering, outlining), write a first draft, revise your draft as many times as necessary, edit your work, and write a final, polished paragraph.

In your drafts, you may rephrase the topic sentence as neces-sary. Using the paragraph on pages 18–19 (showing Magic Johnson as a shooter, passer, rebounder, and leader) as a model, divide your topic into whatever qualities make your subject an excellent ex-ample of whichever type of person you have chosen.

✳ Writer's Guidelines at a Glance: Writing, Revising, and Editing

1. **Write the rough draft.** Referring to your outline for guidance and to your topic sentence for limits, write a first, or rough, draft. Do not get caught up in correcting and polishing your writing during this stage.

2. **Revise.** Mark and revise your rough draft, rewriting as many times as necessary to produce an effective paragraph. The main points of revision are contained in the acronym CLUESS, ex-pressed here as questions.

   Coherence: Does the material flow smoothly from each idea to the next?

   Language: Are the words appropriate for the message, occa-sion, and audience?

   Unity: Are all the ideas related to and subordinate to the topic sentence?

   Emphasis: Have you used techniques such as repetition and placement of ideas to emphasize your main point(s)?

   Support: Have you presented material to back up, justify, or prove your topic sentence?

   Sentences: Have you used some variety of structure and avoided fragments, comma splices, and run-ons?

3. **Edit.** Examine your work carefully. Look for problems in capital-ization, omissions, punctuation, and spelling (COPS).

4. Consider using the Writing Process Worksheet on page xx.

Narration: Moving
Through Time

✳ Writing Paragraphs of Narration

In our everyday lives, we tell stories and invite other people to do so by asking questions such as "What happened at work today?" and "What did you do last weekend?" We are disappointed when the answer is "Nothing much." We may be equally disappointed when a person doesn't give us enough details or gives us too many and spoils the effect. After all, we are interested in people's stories and in the people who tell them. We like narratives.

What is a narrative? A **narrative** is an account of an incident or a series of incidents that make up a complete and significant action. A narrative can be as short as a joke, as long as a novel, or anything in between, including a single paragraph. Each narrative has five properties.

Situation

Situation is the background for the action. The situation may be described only briefly, or it may even be implied. ("To celebrate my seventeenth birthday, I went to the Department of Motor Vehicles to take my practical test for my driver's license.")

Conflict

Conflict is friction, such as a problem in the surroundings, with another person(s), or within the individual. The conflict, which is at the heart of each story, produces struggle. ("It was raining and my appointment was the last one of the day. The examiner was a serious, weary-looking man who reminded me of a bad boss I once had, and I was nervous.")

Struggle

Struggle, which need not be physical, is the manner of dealing with the conflict. The struggle adds action or engagement and generates the plot. ("After grinding on the ignition because the engine was already on, I had trouble finding the windshield wiper control. Next I forgot to signal until after I had pulled away from the curb. As we crept slowly down the rain-glazed street, the examiner told me to take the emergency brake off. All the while I listened to his pen scratching on his clipboard. 'Pull over and park,' he said solemnly.")

Outcome

Outcome is the result of the struggle. ("After I parked the car, the examiner told me to relax, and then he talked to me about school. When we continued, somehow I didn't make any errors, and I got my license.")

Meaning

Meaning is the significance of the story, which may be deeply philosophical or simple, stated or implied ("calmness promotes calmness").

These components are present in some way in all the many forms of the narrative. They are enhanced by the use of various devices like the following:

- **Description** (the use of specific details to advance action, with images to make readers see, smell, taste, hear, and feel)

  the *rain-glazed street*

  listened to his *pen scratching*

- **Dialogue** (the exact words of the speakers, enclosed in quotation marks)

  "*Pull over and park,*" he said solemnly.

- **Transitional words** (words, such as *after, finally, following, later, next, soon,* and *when,* that move a story forward, for narratives are usually presented in chronological order)

  Next I forgot to

  After I parked the car,

Most narratives written as college assignments have an expository purpose (that is, they explain a specified idea). Often the narrative will be merely an extended example. Therefore, the meaning of the narrative is exceedingly important and should be clear, whether it is stated or implied.

☀ Examining Paragraphs of Narration

Student Writers

King of Klutziness

Joel Bailey

We begin with a humorous paragraph by student writer Joel Bailey, who gives an account of his clumsiness as a worker in a fast-food establishment.

Topic sentence   It was my first task of what would be a
memorable day at work in Carl's Jr., a fast-
food place by Universal Studio near
Hollywood. I was assigned to the front
Situation   counter because another worker was late.
There I was at noon, the busiest time of the
day, with no training, scared, and nervous.
In the beginning, things went well. Orders
were routine, and I filled them and made
change. As time passed, the lines got short,
and I was still doing great because, after
all, the job didn't require the mentality of
a rocket scientist. Several counter people
left their registers to help out in back.
Conflict   Then a lot of people came in at one time.
Only two of us were taking orders. I was
nervous. I served three persons, hardly

looking up as I punched the keys, called out orders, and made change. After barely glancing at the next person, I heard his voice ordering, a familiar voice. It was Alex Benson, a reporter for a TV channel I frequently watched. I repeated his order so it would be perfect, and I took his money. After I gave him his change, he stared at the

Struggle receipt and said with more than a touch of irritation, "You made a mistake. You charged me for two chicken burgers." I apologized and gave him a refund. "What about the tax," he growled. "You didn't refund the tax." I was really getting nervous. He always laughed and smiled on TV. I gave him the tax money. I grabbed someone else's chicken order just so I could give him quick service, but when I handed him the tray, my hand slipped and I spilled his Coke on his trousers. Quickly I

Outcome grabbed a napkin and ran around the counter and wiped at the Coke stain. Unfortunately the napkin I grabbed had catsup on it. Now I had added a condiment to the Coke stain. By that time I might as well have salted and peppered him. Beyond anger, and looking

Meaning at me wildly, he fled with his tray to a distant booth and sat with his back to the wall. I decided not to ask for an autograph.

Exercise 1   Discussion and Critical Thinking

1. Is Bailey really klutzy or is this just first-day jitters?

2. Is Bailey's problem with understanding the restaurant's procedures or with executing the procedures?

3. Was this a funny situation at the time?

4. How does the conflict differ from the struggle?

A Moment in the Sun

Karen Bradley

Often the difference between star athletes and others is that the star athletes more consistently make the outstanding plays. In this narrative, student Karen Bradley tells of that one moment when she was a star.

Topic sentence   One event in my childhood stands out clearly in my memory and becomes even stronger as I grow older. When I was eleven years old, I wanted to be a great softball player. Unfortunately for me and my ambition, I was only a bit above average in ability and was smaller than my peers. That didn't

Situation   keep me from becoming catcher on a Lassie League team called the Ripping Rodents. Like me, our team was about average in competition. As we approached the last game of the season, I was batting seventh, and we were fourth in a league of seven teams.

Conflict   The team we were playing, the much-dreaded

Hotshot Hornets, needed this win to take the league championship. Their players were cocky and boastful before the game. They even made rodent jokes. Then they walked by our dugout after taking infield practice and acted as if we were not there. Finally they posed for some pictures a parent was taking; they even had a sign saying "2A Lassie League Champions." For the first time all year we were angry--at them, at ourselves. And then we went on to surprise ourselves. In the last inning with them at bat, we were leading by one run. After their first two batters made outs, the next one, a speedy, little second

Struggle baseman named Toni, walked. Everyone knew she would try to steal second. She was the fastest player in the league and had never been thrown out. On the first pitch she took off. The ball was shoulder-high to me. I grabbed it out of my glove and threw it as hard as I could in the direction of second base. To my surprise, and even more so to Toni's, the ball went on a low arc right to our shortstop, knee-high.

Outcome Toni slid, but she was out by three feet. The game was over, and the Ripping Rodents were all over me. It was as if we had won the championship. It was my only moment of stardom

Meaning in softball, but it will do.

Exercise 2 Discussion and Critical Thinking

1. How does Bradley's not being an All Star player on an ordinary team make this paragraph more dramatic?

2. Why does Bradley remember the incident so well?

3. How important is it for people to have these special moments?

4. How much does Bradley reveal about herself?

Professional Writer

Voice Like Twigs Underfoot

Maxine Hong Kingston

> *Now a celebrated writer, Maxine Hong Kingston was once so deficient in English speech that she flunked kindergarten. In this passage taken from her book* The Woman Warrior: Memoirs of a Childhood Among Ghosts *(1976), she tells about one of her early experiences as a frightened girl caught between two cultures.*

Not all of the children who were silent at American school found voice at Chinese school.* One new teacher said each of us had to get up and recite in front of the class, who was to listen. My sister and I had memorized the lesson perfectly. We said it to each other at home, one chanting, one listening. The teacher called on my sister to recite first. It was the first time a teacher had called on the second-born to go first. My sister was scared. She glanced at me and looked away; I looked down at my desk. I hoped that she could do it because if she could, then I would have to. She opened her mouth and a voice came out that wasn't a whisper, but it wasn't a proper voice either. I hoped that she would not cry, fear breaking up her voice like twigs underfoot. She sounded as if she were trying to sing through weeping and strangling. She did not pause to stop to end the embarrassment. She kept going until she said the last word, and then she sat

---

*Kingston attended both the public American school and the private Chinese school.

down. When it was my turn, the same voice came out, a crippled animal running on broken legs. You could hear splinters in my voice, bones rubbing jagged against one another. I was loud, though. I was glad I didn't whisper.

Exercise 3 Discussion and Critical Thinking

In your own words, identify the following parts of Kingston's narrative.

Situation: _____

_____

Conflict: _____

_____

Struggle: _____

_____

Outcome: _____

_____

Meaning: _____

_____

☀ Practicing Patterns of Narration

Exercise 4 Completing Patterns

Fill in the blanks to complete each narrative pattern.

1. Lost and Found

   (situation)   I. Person taking store money deposit bag to bank

   (conflict)   II. Person loses bag

   (struggle)   III. _____

   (outcome)   IV. _____

   (meaning)   V. _____

2. Good Samaritan

(situation)	I. Driver with flat tire, dead of night
(conflict)	II. No spare tire
(struggle)	III. _____
(outcome)	IV. _____
(meaning)	V. _____

✳ Topics for Paragraphs of Narration

Reading-Related Topics

"King of Klutziness"

1. Write a narrative paragraph about learning how to do something specific on the job. In what way(s) did you or someone else perform badly, perhaps ridiculously? Many of these events occur on the first day of employment.

"A Moment in the Sun"

2. Write about a time when you exceeded expectations in a sport or in another endeavor such as work, family life, school, or a social situation.
3. Discuss the properties of this long paragraph about Bradley's special moment. What factors made this special? Refer directly to the selection as you analyze it.
4. Use your imagination to write about this incident from the point of view of Toni (the speedster who was thrown out).

"Voice Like Twigs Underfoot"

5. Write a narrative paragraph about something you had to struggle to do, like make a presentation or talk to someone you admired, held in high esteem, or were afraid of.

Cross-Curricular Topics

6. Write a case study of an individual's behavior: in a class requiring observation, such as teacher training, physical education, sociology, psychology, or business management.

7. Write a report on how you completed an experiment in a class (biology, ecology, psychology).

8. Describe a pivotal moment or revealing incident in the life of a historical figure, a composer, an artist, an author.

Career-Related Topics

9. Write a narrative paragraph about a work-related encounter between a manager and a worker, and briefly explain the significance of the event.

10. Write a narrative paragraph about an encounter between a customer and a salesperson. Explain what went right and wrong.

11. Write a narrative paragraph about how a person solved a work-related problem.

12. Write a narrative paragraph about a salesperson's dealing with a customer's complaint. Critique the procedure.

General Topics

13. Write a narrative paragraph about a personal experience that you might characterize as the most amusing, sad, terrifying, satisfying, stupid, rewarding, self-centered, generous, stingy, loving, thoughtful, cruel, regrettable, educational, corrupting, sinful, virtuous, or disgusting thing you have done or witnessed. Keep in mind that you are writing about a single event or a portion of that event.

14. Write a narrative paragraph about the first time you did something, such as the first time you dated, kissed romantically, spoke formally in public, entered a new school, worked for pay, drove an automobile, rode a bicycle or motorcycle, danced, received a traffic citation, met a celebrity, or played a game.

✳ Writer's Guidelines at a Glance: Narration

1. Use this checklist to be sure you have a complete narrative.

☐ Situation (at beginning)
☐ Conflict
☐ Struggle
☐ Outcome
☐ Meaning

2. Use these devices as appropriate:

- Images (sight, sound, smell, taste, touch) and other details to advance action
- Dialogue
- Transitional words (such as *after, finally, following, later, next, soon, when*) to enhance chronological order

✳ 5

Description: Moving Through Space and Time

✳ Writing Paragraphs of Description

Description is the use of words to represent the appearance or nature of something. Often called a **word picture,** description attempts to present its subject for the mind's eye. In doing so, it does not merely become an indifferent camera; instead, it selects details that will depict something well. Just what details the descriptive writer selects will depend on several factors, especially the type of description and the dominant impression in the passage.

Types of Description

On the basis of treatment of subject material, description is customarily divided into two types: objective and subjective.

Effective **objective description** presents the subject clearly and directly as it exists outside the realm of feelings. If you are explaining the function of the heart, the characteristics of a computer chip, or the renovation of a manufacturing facility, your description would probably feature specific, impersonal details. Most technical and scientific writing is objective in that sense. It is likely to be practical and utilitarian, making little use of speculation and poetic technique while focusing on details of sight.

Effective **subjective description** is also concerned with clarity and it may be direct, but it conveys a feeling about the subject and sets a mood while making a point. Because most expression involves personal views, even when it explains by analysis, subjective description (often called **emotional description**) has a broader range of uses than objective description.

Descriptive passages can have a combination of objective and subjective description; only the larger context of the passage will reveal the main intent.

Imagery

To convey your main concern effectively to readers, you will have to give some sensory impressions. These sensory impressions, collectively called **imagery,** refer to that which can be experienced by the senses—what we can see, smell, taste, hear, and touch.

Subjective description is more likely to use images and words rich in associations than is objective description. But just as a fine line cannot always be drawn between the objective and the subjective, a fine line cannot always be drawn between word choice in one and in the other. However, we can say with certainty that whatever the type of description, careful word choice will always be important.

General and Specific Words

To move from the general to the specific is to move from the whole class or body to the individual(s); for example:

General	Specific	More Specific
food	pastry	Twinkie
mess	grease	oil slicks on table
drink	soda	mug of root beer
odor	smell from grill	smell of frying onions

Abstract and Concrete Words

Words are classified as abstract or concrete depending on what they refer to. **Abstract words** refer to qualities or ideas: *good, ordinary, ultimate, truth, beauty, maturity, love.* **Concrete words** refer to substances or things; they have reality: *onions, grease, buns, tables, food.* The specific concrete words, sometimes called **concrete particulars,** often support generalizations effectively and convince the reader of the accuracy of the account.

Dominant Impression

Never try to give all of the details in description; instead, be selective, picking only those that you need to make a dominant impression, always taking into account the knowledge and attitudes of your readers. Remember, description is not photographic. If you wish to describe a person, select only those traits that will present the person according to your concerns. If you wish to describe a landscape, do not give all the details that you might find in a photo; just pick the details that support what you want to say. That extremely important dominant impression is directly linked to your purpose and is created by choosing and arranging images and other revealing details.

Order: Time and Space

All of these details must have some order. Time and space are the main controlling factors in most description.

If you were describing something that was not changing—a room, for example—you would be concerned with space and give directions to the reader such as *next to, below, under, above, behind, in front of, beyond, in the foreground, in the background, to the left,* or *to the right.*

If you were describing something that was changing, such as a butterfly going through metamorphosis, you would be concerned mainly with time and use transitional words such as *first, second, then, soon, finally, while, after, next, later, now,* or *before.*

If you were walking through an area—so that the setting was changing—you would use both time and space for order.

Procedure at a Glance

What is your subject? (school campus during summer vacation)

What is the dominant impression? (deserted)

What details support the dominant impression?

1. (smell of flowers and cut grass rather than food and smoke and perfume)
2. (dust accumulated on white porcelain drinking fountain)
3. (sound of the wind, wildlife, and silence rather than people)
4. (crunch of dead leaves underfoot)
5. (echo of footsteps)

What is the situation? (You are walking across the campus in early August.)

What is the order of details? (time and place)

✳ Examining Paragraphs of Description

Student Writers

The Santa Anas

Juanita Rivera

For her descriptive paragraph, Juanita Rivera chose to write about something she has experienced many times, the fierce and dreaded windstorms—the Santa Anas—that come howling from the desert into her Los Angeles neighborhood.

In the L.A. Basin, people know why the Santa Anas are called the "devil winds." They come in from the desert searing hot like the breath of a blast furnace, tumbling over the mountain ranges and streaking down the canyons. Pitilessly they destroy and disrupt. Trees are stripped of foliage, broken, and toppled. Fires that start in the foothills may become fire storms and bombard the downwind areas with smoke, ash, and burning embers. But even without fire, the winds pick up sand, dirt, and debris and send them toward the ocean as a hot, dry, dirty tide going out. All the time, the Santa Anas are relentless, humming, howling, and whining through yards, and rattling and rippling loose shingles. Palm fronds slap and clatter. Dogs howl and often panic and run away; birds hunker down in wind breaks; and human beings

```
mostly stay inside, wiping up the dust,

coughing, and getting grumpy. The devil winds

earn their reputation.
```

Exercise 1 Discussion and Critical Thinking

1. Double underline the topic sentence and the concluding sentence.

2. What is the dominant impression?

3. Underline the supporting images.

4. Of the five images—sight, sound, taste, touch, smell—which two are used most in this paragraph?

5. Is the order of presentation based on time, space, or both time and space?

```
                    My Burning Scarf

                      Julie Lee
```

Student Julie Lee writes about a scarf that was mistakenly burned in a family ceremony. Her attention to descriptive detail highlights this vivid recollection and conveys the poignancy of her experience.

```
                During my childhood, my favorite

              possession was the yellow scarf my dad gave

              me when I was five. It would bring me

Topic
sentence      pleasure and pain. Hand-sewn with care in

              Japan, it attracted many curious and envious

              eyes. Needless to say, I was the proud owner
```

of that scarf and loved the attention it
brought me. The scarf was about two feet
square and made of pure virgin wool. It was
decorated with a fringed green edge, and in
one corner five embroidered yellow-colored
chicks played against the background
needlework of lush green grass. The material
was as soft as cashmere and had the warmth of
fur. It kept my cheeks warm when I wrapped it
loosely around my neck. But when I was six, I
let my seriously ill sister wear my scarf to
the doctor's office. She didn't give it back
to me immediately and, because she was sick,
I didn't ask for it. Sadly, she died of
leukemia after months of suffering. A few
days after she died, from my bedroom, I saw
my mother in the backyard burning personal
items that belonged to my dead sister. It is
the Korean custom to do so. My mother was
crying and so were other adults standing in a
circle around the fire. Then I saw my mother
pick up my wadded yellow scarf and shake it
out. I rushed outside, shrieking for her to
stop. Over the sounds of sobbing and the
popping of the fire, I wanted to shout,
"That's my scarf, my precious possession."
But I didn't, and my mother, thinking I was
crying only for my sister, flung it into the

```
flames of the fire that popped and cracked,

and the green and yellow of my childhood

turned to orange, then red, then gray.
```

Exercise 2 Discussion and Critical Thinking

1. What two words from the topic sentence provide the dominant impression?

2. In the left margin, annotate the images of sight, touch, and sound.

3. Lee looks back almost fifteen years to an experience. In what ways is her recollection clearly that of a six or seven year old?


```
                    The Drag

                 Mike Kavanagh
```

When student Mike Kavanagh looked at the assignment to write a descriptive paragraph about something he knew well, he had no trouble selecting a subject. As a drag racer for sport and prize money, he had built up his car, a 1968 Camaro, to thunder down the track at more than two hundred miles per hour, with all his senses raw to the wind.

Topic sentence
```
                    As I climb into the cockpit for my drag,

          I hear the roar of the crowd and the

          thundering blasts in the background. Engulfed

          in an iron cage, I strap myself down. First

          over the shoulders, then from the waist, and

          finally from between my legs the straps merge

          and then buckle at my belly button. This is

          to ensure my stability in the ironclad, two-
```

hundred-and-thirty-miles-per-hour street
rocket. My crew then signals me to fire up
the three thousand horsepower motor mounted
at my back. With the push of a button, I feel
the rumble of the motor, hear the scream of
the blower, and smell the distinctive odor of
nitro in the air. I then move up to the
starting line to dry hop my rear tires for

Description and narrative frame

better traction. I quickly thrust the
accelerator pedal to the floor. I am shot
forward about two hundred feet. Letting off
the accelerator pedal and pulling the brake
handle allows me to come to a slow stop. A
low continuous thump from the motor echoes
through my head as I reverse back to the
starting line. As I creep forward, I stage
the beast and wait for the lights to change
to green. This feels like an eternity. The
lights flicker yellow, yellow, yellow, GREEN!
I stab the pedal to the floor. I am flung
thirteen hundred and twenty feet faster than
I can say my name. When I pull the brake and
parachute handles simultaneously, I lunge
back from the force of the billowing chutes.
I climb out of the jungle gym and look up at
the scoreboard, which reads 5.26 seconds at

Concluding sentence

230.57. There's nothing else like rocketing
down the track at that speed!

Exercise 3 Discussion and Critical Thinking

1. Is this paragraph mainly descriptive, mainly narrative, or equally balanced?

2. Annotate in the margin and underline at least one image of sound, sight, touch, and smell.

3. Although you probably have not drag raced competitively, you can get a good sense of what it is like to do so by reading this paragraph. What details and what phrasing convince you that Kavanagh is writing from experience?

4. What is the dominant impression?

Professional Writer

The Mousetrap

Craig Finley

> *Freelance writer Craig Finley begins this paragraph with a stark description of the mousetrap and then dispassionately explains its function. In his clear and concise presentation, the paragraph is as practical, effective, and impersonal as the object it depicts.*

The mousetrap is a remarkably simple and efficient instrument. The platform is a rectangular piece of soft pine wood, two and a half inches wide, six inches long, and a quarter-inch thick. The plane surface of the piece of wood is evenly divided by a square strike bar, which is attached to the middle by three staples. The staples are evenly spaced, with one in the middle. Between the middle and end staples on each side is a strong metal spring coiled around the bar. Each spring is taut and kept that way by the use of a straight piece of metal thrust out from the coil and tucked up under the kill bar on one side and placed against the board on the other. Also attached to the center kill bar is a bait pad, a little rectangular piece of flat metal with a grooved edge extending up from one side to hold the trigger rod. At the open end of the board, from an eye-screw, dangles the trigger rod, a long piece of metal that can move freely in a half circle from a point behind the screw to the grooved bait pad. To set the trap, place the bait, preferably cheese, on the bait pad, then cock the kill bar by pulling the free end over in a half circle to the other side and tucking it under the trigger rod. Then secure the kill bar by moving the trigger rod into the groove on the side of the bait pad. When the rodent nibbles on the cheese, it will move the bait pad, which will loosen the trigger rod and, in turn, release the kill bar in its fatal arc to pin the rodent against the board.

Exercise 4   Discussion and Critical Thinking

1. Underline the topic sentence.

2. Is the description objective or subjective? Explain.

3. Write an X to mark the spot where description becomes an explanation of how the mousetrap works.

4. Use phrases from the description to label the ten parts of the drawing on page 67. If you are artistically inclined, add a rodent.

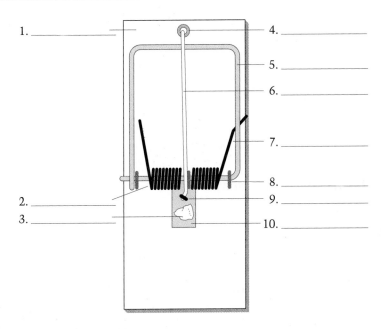

1. _____

2. _____

3. _____

4. _____

5. _____

6. _____

7. _____

8. _____

9. _____

10. _____

✳ **Practicing Patterns of Description**

Exercise 5 Completing Patterns

Fill in the blanks in the following outline to complete the description.

A Produce Area in a Supermarket
(Dominant impression: Diversity)

I. Food displays (sight—color, shape)

    A. _____

    B. _____

    C. _____

II. Smells (from vegetables, fruits)

    A. _____

    B. _____

III. Textures (smooth or rough to touch)

   A. _____

   B. _____

IV. Taste (samples of sweet/sour, ripe/unripe)

   A. _____

   B. _____

✳ Topics for Paragraphs of Description

Reading-Related Topics

"The Santa Anas"

1. Describe a characteristic of the weather that has or has had a dramatic influence on your community. It might be a chinook, tornado, hurricane, blizzard, dust storm, flood, or drought.

"My Burning Scarf"

2. Write a highly descriptive paragraph about a possession you received or purchased, treasured, and—somehow—lost, through theft, your gift-giving, or someone's neglect. Describe it well, but locate the possession in the framework of a little story.

"The Drag"

3. Describe an exciting moment you experienced; it need not be a sporting event, but it can be. It could be an accident, a rescue, an unexpected pleasure, or any personal triumph. Pick an event you can describe colorfully.

"The Mousetrap"

4. Describe a simple item and explain how it functions. Consider items such as a yo-yo, a Slinky, a flashlight, a pair of scissors, nail clippers, a pocket knife, a baby bottle, a diaper, a music box, a windup toy, a broom, a special wrench, or a can opener. Consider using an illustration.

Cross-Curricular Topics

5. Use description in one of the following assignments.

- Agriculture: Field-trip report
- Art History: Report on a museum or a particular work of art
- Education: School-visit report
- Ecology: Field-trip report
- Geology: Field-trip report
- Sociology: Report on a field trip to an urban zone, a prison, or another institution

Career-Related Topics

6. Describe a well-furnished, well-functioning office or other work area. Be specific.
7. Describe a product, with special attention to the dominant trait that gives the product its reputation.
8. Describe a specific person properly groomed and attired for a particular job or interview. Be specific in giving details pertaining to the person and in naming the place or situation. If you like, objectively describe yourself as that specific person.

General Topics
Objective Description

Give your topic some kind of frame. As you develop your purpose, consider the knowledge and attitudes of your readers. You might be describing a lung for a biology instructor, a geode for a geology instructor, a painting for an art instructor, or a comet for an astronomy instructor. Or maybe you could pose as the seller of an object such as a desk, a table, or a bicycle. Try some of the following topics:

9. A simple object, such as a pencil, a pair of scissors, a cup, a sock, a dollar bill, a coin, a ring, or a notebook.
10. A human organ, such as a heart, a liver, a lung, or a kidney.
11. A visible part of your body, such as a toe, a finger, an ear, a nose, or an eye.
12. A construction, such as a room, a desk, a chair, a table.
13. A mechanism, such as a bicycle, a tricycle, a wagon, a car, a motorcycle, a can opener, or a stapler.

Subjective Description

The following topics should also be presented in the context of a purpose other than just writing a description. Your intent can be as simple as giving a subjective reaction to your subject. But unless you are dealing with one of those topics that you can present reflectively or a topic interesting in itself, you will usually need some kind of situation. The narrative frame (something happening) is especially useful in providing order and vitality for writing. Here are two possibilities for you to consider.

14. Personalize a trip to a supermarket, a stadium, an airport, an unusual house, a mall, a beach, a court, a place of worship, a club, a business, a library, or a police station. Deal with a simple conflict in one of those places, while emphasizing descriptive details.

15. Pick a high point in any event, and describe a few seconds of it. Think about how a scene can be captured by a video camera, and then give focus by applying the dominant-impression principle, using the images of sight, sound, taste, touch, and smell that are relevant. The event might be a ball game, a graduation ceremony, a wedding ceremony, a funeral, a dance, a concert, a family gathering, a class meeting, a rally, a riot, a robbery, a fight, a proposal, or a meal. Focus on a body of subject material that you can cover effectively in the paragraph you write.

✳ Writer's Guidelines at a Glance: Description

1. In an **objective description,** use direct, practical language and usually appeal mainly to the sense of sight.
2. In an **emotional description,** appeal to the reader's feelings, especially through the use of images of sight, sound, smell, taste, and touch.
3. Use specific and concrete words if appropriate.
4. Be sure that readers can answer the following questions:

> What is the subject of this description?
> What is the dominant impression?
> What is the situation?
> What is the order of details—time, space, or both?
> What details support the dominant impression?

Exemplification: Writing with Examples

✳ Writing Paragraphs of Exemplification

Exemplification means using examples to explain, convince, or amuse. Lending interest and information to writing, exemplification is one of the most common and effective ways of developing ideas. Examples may be developed in a sentence or more, or they may be only phrases or even single words, as in the following sentence: "Children like packaged breakfast foods, such as *Wheaties, Cheerios,* and *Rice Krispies.*"

Characteristics of Good Examples

As supporting information, the best examples are vivid, specific, and representative. These three qualities are closely linked, and collectively, they must support the topic sentence. The **vivid** example attracts attention. Then through a memorable presentation and the use of identifying names, the example becomes **specific** to the reader. A good example must also be **representative;** that is, it must be experienced as typical so that it can be the basis for a generalization.

Finally, and most important, the connection between the example and the topic sentence must be clear. A bizarre case of cheating may be fascinating in itself (vivid and specific), but to be effective in a paragraph on "the hard work of cheating," it must also support the topic sentence. The reader should say, in effect, "That's interesting, convincing, and memorable. Though it's unusual, I can see that it's typical of what goes on."

Techniques for Finding Examples

Writing a good paragraph of exemplification begins, as always, with prewriting. The techniques you use will depend on what you are writing about. Assuming that you begin with a topic idea, one useful technique is listing. Base your list on what you have read, heard, and experienced. Here is a list on the broad topic "cheating at school":

> When I copied homework
> Looking at a friend's test answers
> A student with hand signals
> Jake and his electronic system
> Time for planned cheating
> Those who got caught
> A person who bought a research paper
> Jess, who copied from me
> The Internet "Cheaters" source
> The two students who exchanged identities
> More work than it's worth
> More stress than it's worth

Connecting Examples with Purpose

Here is the final paragraph on the topic "the hard work of cheating."

Topic sentence	Cheating students often put themselves under more stress than honest students. I
Extended example	remember someone in my junior composition class who needed a research paper, so he found a source and bought one for seventy-five dollars. The first trouble was that he had to submit the work in stages: the topic, the working bibliography, the note cards, the outline, the rough draft, and the final. Therefore, he went to the library and started working backwards. Of course, he couldn't

turn in only the bib cards actually used in

the paper, and next he had to make out note

cards for the material he "would be"

documenting, and even make out more. After

having all kinds of trouble, he realized that

the bought paper was of "A" quality, whereas

he had been a "C" student. He went back to

his source and was told he should change the

sentence structure and so on to make the

paper weaker. Finally he dropped the class

after spending more time on his paper than I

Concluding   did on mine. He also suffered more anxiety
sentence

than the students who put in the most work on

their papers.

✳ Examining Paragraphs of Exemplification

Student Writer

Sweet and Sour Workplace

Sarah Betrue

*A full-time student and a full-time worker, Sarah Betrue has a
very busy life, which would go more smoothly if she did not have
so many irritations. We are likely to identify with her experiences and to admire her for beginning and ending her work day
in tranquility.*

Every morning as I enter my workplace, I
admire the vibrant colors of both the
tropical fish in the aquarium and the ancient
silk Chinese robes hung from the wall. But as
I take the dreaded step from the dining area
to the kitchen, the scenery drastically

Topic
sentence
changes. Stressful and frustrating situations
occur daily behind the scenes at the
restaurant, making it almost impossible for
me to maintain a positive attitude. Consider

Example
yesterday as a typical shift. The first
voices I hear are the owners complaining
about how filthy the restaurant looks,
although the night before, the other employees
and I worked with Ajax for three hours
scrubbing shelves and floor sinks. As the day
progresses, I try to squeeze in some extra
cleaning between busy times, but I find
myself doing all the extra work myself. The
young girls I work with think having this job
is just an extension of their social lives.
During lunch hour, the dining area is packed,
the line for takeout has reached a ridiculous
length, and two phone calls are on hold.

Example
That's when Morgan decides to call her
boyfriend on her cell phone. Naturally I
become frustrated and proceed to speak with

her. She glares at me with fire in her eyes and screams, "I've got more important things to deal with at this time!" Getting nowhere with politeness, I grab the phone from her hand and turn it off. No sooner has this crisis ended than the house phone rings

Example again. <u>On the line is a very unhappy woman.</u> After listening to a few colorfully disparaging descriptions of a meal she ordered, I tell her I cannot give refunds or food exchanges if her order is not returned first. She threatens to report our restaurant to newspapers and authorities, and then tells me to do something I am physically incapable of doing and hangs up in my ear. At the end of the day I am so angry and frustrated with having to put up with such occurrences that I want to grab hold of one of the woks and whack someone upside the head. But just as I reach for the handle, I get a vision, an image of

Concluding my paycheck, and I begin to relax. <u>I leave</u>
sentence <u>the restaurant with no blood on my hands,</u> <u>wishing everyone a wonderful evening.</u>

Exercise 1 Discussion and Critical Thinking

1. What evidence shows that Betrue is not essentially a negative thinker?

2. What kind of order does Betrue use for her three specific supporting examples?

3. If you were one of the owners of the restaurant, how would you react to Betrue's paragraph?

Professional Writers

When Cupid Aims at the Workplace

Harvey R. Meyer

> *Freelance author Harvey R. Meyer uses specific examples to show how romance can cause problems at the workplace. This paragraph is taken from Meyer's essay published in* Nation's Business. *The examples are set off by bullets, following a common format for presenting support information in business writing.*

Romances between co-workers can cause problems for a company. Owners and managers should be prepared to handle such situations as these:

- At a small Midwestern company, a flowering romance between a married but separated partner in the firm and a single secretary sparked a furor among the two other partners. The office atmosphere became so strained that the secretary was terminated and the stunned middle-aged partner was forced out. He had to start a competing business from scratch.

- The controller of a small company in the Southeast and a warehouseman made no bones about their adulterous relationship, kissing and pawing each other ostentatiously. The two eventually left their spouses and married. But the warehouseman soon took advantage of his new wife's high standing in the company, overstepping his authority and, unbeknown to her, sexually harassing female workers. Fed up, the owner told the controller that her husband was being fired for those abuses, whereupon both spouses angrily quit and threatened to capsize the firm.

As these real-life cases illustrate, love—though it may be a many-splendored thing—can have devastating consequences in small firms. Depending on the situation, office love affairs can wreak havoc on morale, productivity, and even the bottom line. Some workplace romances can even lead to sexual harassment charges against a company. Although firms probably can't and shouldn't try to stop love in the workplace, they should take steps to protect themselves and ensure that the work environment is healthy, professional, and productive.

Exercise 2 Discussion and Critical Thinking

1. Underline the topic sentence.

2. Underline the concluding sentence.

3. The subject of this paragraph is romances. What is the next most important word?

4. The examples pertain mainly to management and they support the view that the company's stability may be in jeopardy if romances develop. Do you think Meyer would hold essentially the same view toward labor-only romances?

5. If a labor-only romance were to interfere with workplace efficiency, what would management probably do?

Colorado Springs—Every Which Way

Eric Schlosser

In his best-selling book Fast Food Nation, *Eric Schlosser exposes an ignorant and largely uncaring society dependent on fast food. At the end of unsavory supply lines are rudderless cities thickly populated by fast food chains serving up unhealthful food. One such city is Colorado Springs.*

Colorado Springs now has the feel of a city whose identity is not yet fixed. Many longtime residents strongly oppose the extremism of the newcomers, sporting bumper stickers that say, "Don't Californicate Colorado." The city is now torn between opposing visions of what America should be. Colorado Springs has twenty-eight Charismatic Christian churches and almost twice as many pawnbrokers, a Lord's Vineyard Bookstore and a First Amendment Adult Bookstore, a Christian Medical and Dental Society and a Holey Rollers Tattoo Parlor. It has a Christian summer camp whose founder, David Noebel, outlined the dangers of rock 'n' roll in his pamphlet *Communism, Hypnotism, and the Beatles.* It has a gay entertainment complex called The Hide & Seek, where the Gay Rodeo Association meets. It has a public school principal who recently disciplined a group of sixth-grade girls for reading a book on witchcraft and allegedly casting spells. The loopiness once associated with Los Angeles has come full-blown to Colorado Springs—the strange, creative energy that crops up where the future's consciously being made, where people walk the fine line separating a visionary from a total nutcase. At the start of a new century, all sorts of things seem possible there. The cultural and the physical landscapes of Colorado Springs are up for grabs.

Exercise 3   Discussion and Critical Thinking

1. Underline the two sentences that focus on Schlosser's main idea.

2. Of the two sentences, which one is directly tied to most of the examples?

3. Circle each example that supports the idea in the third sentence. Notice that most appear in contrasting patterns.

4. How does the last sentence function as part of the paragraph structure?

5. Do you know of other cities that are "torn between opposing visions of what America should be"? If so, give examples to support your contention.

✳ Practicing Patterns of Exemplification

Completing Patterns

Fill in the blanks in the following outlines to add more examples that support the topic sentences.

1. Topic sentence: Just walking through my favorite mall [or shopping center] shows me that the world is smaller than it used to be.

    I. People of different cultures (with specific examples)

    II. Foods of different cultures (with specific examples)

    III. _____

    IV. _____

2. Topic sentence: Driving to work [or school] this month and observing the behavior of other drivers have convinced me that road rage has invaded my community.

    I. A man honking his horn impatiently at an elderly driver

    II. _____

    III. _____

✳ Topics for Paragraphs of Exemplification

Reading-Related Topics

"Sweet and Sour Workplace"

1. With this selection as a model, use examples to develop your ideas on how you have experienced and dealt with irritation at school, home, or work.

2. With this selection as a model, use examples to write about irritations in a neighborhood; in theaters during a movie; on airplanes, buses, or trains; on streets, highways, and freeways; or in restaurants.

"When Cupid Aims at the Workplace"

3. Using this paragraph as a model for writing about workplace romances you have observed, explain how they have created an atmosphere of perceived favoritism or have created uncomfortable working conditions. Consider concluding by commenting on what was done or what should have been done.

"Colorado Springs—Every Which Way"

4. Using this paragraph as a model of development by examples, write about a similar city, one that exhibits contradictory features of products, services, and individual behavior.
5. Referring to clubs, activities, and course offerings, discuss how a college you are familiar with is torn between opposing visions of what America should be.

Cross-Curricular Topics

Use examples to write paragraphs for these following assignments.

6. Tests or similar written assignments: Include supporting information, either specific or extended examples.
7. Reports: Focus on one or more examples as representative of a much larger group; for example, a focused discussion of one work of art in a museum grouping of pieces by style or a study of a particular typical student in a class visit for an education class.

Career-Related Topics

Use specific examples to support one of the following statements as applied to business or work:

8. It's not what you know, it's who you know.
9. Don't burn your bridges.
10. Like Lego, business is a matter of connections.
11. The customer is always right.
12. Money is honey, my little sonny, and the rich man's joke is always funny.

13. If you take care of the pennies, the dollars will take care of themselves.
14. A kind word turns away wrath.

General Topics

Make a judgmental statement about a social issue you believe in strongly and then use an example or examples to illustrate your point. Some possible topics include the following:

15. The price of groceries is too high.
16. Professional athletes are paid too much.
17. A person buying a new car may get a lemon.
18. Drivers sometimes openly ignore the laws on a selective basis.
19. Politicians should be watched.
20. Working and going to school is tough.
21. Working, parenting, and going to school is tough.

✳ Writer's Guidelines at a Glance: Exemplification

1. Use examples to explain, convince, or amuse.
2. Use examples that are vivid, specific, and representative.

   - Vivid examples attract attention.
   - Specific examples are identifiable.
   - Representative examples are typical and therefore the basis for generalizations.

3. Tie your examples clearly to your topic sentence.
4. Draw your examples from what you have read, heard, and experienced.
5. Brainstorm a list of possible examples before you write.

7

Analysis by Division: Examining the Parts

✳ Writing Paragraphs of Analysis by Division

If you need to explain how something works or exists as a unit, you will write an analysis by division. You will break down a unit (your subject) into its parts and explain how each part functions in relation to the operation or existence of the whole. The most important word here is *unit*. You begin with something that can stand alone or can be regarded separately, such as a poem, a heart, a painting, a car, a bike, a person, a school, or a committee.

The following procedure will guide you in writing an analysis by division. Move from subject to principle, to division, to relationship:

Step 1: Begin with something that is a unit.
Step 2: State one principle by which the unit can function.
Step 3: Divide the unit into parts according to that principle.
Step 4: Discuss each of the parts in relation to the unit.

Here's how this general procedure is applied to a real object (unit).

Step 1: For the unit, we choose a pencil.
Step 2: For the principle, or way of regarding the unit, we see the pencil as a writing instrument.
Step 3: For the division into parts based on the principle of a pencil as a writing instrument, we divide the pencil into an eraser, an eraser holder, a wooden barrel, and a thin graphite core with a sharpened point.
Step 4: For the discussion of parts in relation to the unit, we present the following: "At the top of the wooden barrel is a strip of metal encircling an eraser and clamping it to the barrel. In the center of the barrel is a core of graphite that can be sharpened to a point at the end and used for writing. The eraser is used to remove marks made by the graphite

82

point. Thus we have a complete writing tool, one that marks and erases marks."

Like many things, a pencil can be regarded in different ways. For example, an artist might not consider a pencil mainly as a writing tool. Instead, an artist might look at a pencil and see it as an object that could be used as a subject in a still-life painting. Here is how an artist might follow the procedure:

Step 1: For the unit, I choose a pencil.

Step 2: For the principle or way of regarding the unit, I see the pencil as an object of simple functional beauty.

Step 3: For the division into parts based on my principle, I divide the pencil into texture, shape, and color.

Step 4: For the discussion of parts in relation to the unit, I explain how the textures of the metal, graphite, and wood, along with their shapes and colors, produce a beautiful object.

Either treatment of the same unit, the pencil, is valid, but mixing the treatments by applying more than one principle at a time causes problems. For example, if we were to say that a pencil has an eraser, an eraser holder, a wooden barrel, a graphite core, and a beautiful coat of yellow paint, we would have an illogical analysis by division, because the "beautiful coat of yellow paint" does not relate to the pencil as a writing instrument.

Organization

In a paragraph of analysis by division, the main parts are likely to be the main points of your outline or main extensions of your cluster. If they are anything else, reconsider your organization. For the pencil, your outline might look like this:

I. Eraser
II. Eraser holder
III. Wooden barrel
IV. Graphite core with point at one end

Sequence of Parts

The order in which you discuss the parts will vary according to the nature of the unit and the way in which you view it. Here are some possible sequences for organizing the parts of a unit.

- **Time:** The sequence of the parts in your paragraph can be based on time (if you are dealing with something that functions on its own, such as a heart, with the parts presented in relation to stages of the function).
- **Space:** If your unit is a visual object, especially if, like the pencil, it does nothing by itself, you may discuss the parts in relation to space. In the example of the pencil, the parts of the pencil begin at the top with the eraser and end at the bottom with the pencil point.
- **Emphasis:** Because the most emphatic part of any piece of writing is the end (the second most emphatic point is the beginning), consider placing the most significant part of the unit at the end. In the example, both space and emphasis govern the placement of the pencil point at the end of the order.

✳ Examining Paragraphs of Analysis by Division

Student Writer

More Than Ordinary

Nancy Samuels

Faced with writing on the topic of "an example of a hero, with a discussion of the hero's traits [analysis by division]," Nancy Samuels didn't have to go to the library. Right in her household she found her subject—her mother. She writes about an ordinary person who faced a difficult challenge and succeeded in a situation in which others gave up.

Topic sentence   My mother is the best example of a hero I can think of. No one will read about her in a book about heroes, but in her small circle of friends, no one doubts her heroism. Certainly my younger brother doesn't. He is the special beneficiary of her heroism. He was in an accident when he was five years old, and the doctor told us that he would never walk again. My mother listened respectfully, but

Trait   she didn't believe him. She had <u>optimism</u>. She

went to another doctor and then another.

Finally she found one who prescribed

exercises. She worked with my brother for

three years. Day after dismal day, she

Trait   <u>persevered</u>. It wasn't just her working with

him that helped my brother. It was her raw

courage in the face of failure. My brother

Trait   worked with her. They both were <u>courageous</u>.

We other family members weren't. To us my

brother and mother were acting like a couple

of blind fools. We thought my mother

especially, the leader, was in prolonged

denial. But in three years my brother was

walking. He won't be an athlete;

nevertheless, he gets around. We're proud of

him, but we know--and he knows--that without

Mother he would never have walked. Of course,

she's not a miracle worker. Most of the time,

doctors are right, and some injured people

can never walk. But the ones like my brother,

who somewhere have that hidden ability, need

that special someone like my mother. She's

Concluding
sentence   more than ordinary. <u>She's a hero.</u>

Exercise 1   Discussion and Critical Thinking

1. What are the main traits of Samuels's heroic mother?

2. Is she a miracle worker? Why or why not?

3. Will her kind of strength always succeed? Explain.

4. Would she have been considered heroic if she had not succeeded in helping her son?

Professional Writers

Golden Oldies

Jerry Bratcher

> *Freelance writer Jerry Bratcher reflects on one of our treasured shared experiences. He reminds us that all the songs we call "golden oldies" have common characteristics, and we note that his discussion of those characteristics is an analysis by division.*

Radio stations have made golden oldies their entire program. Television infomercials have beckoned those from a particular oldie period to listen to and buy CD collections. "Golden oldies" has become a term with components familiar to all of us. Anyone can love the songs, but only listeners who were around to hear them first can truly cherish all their dimensions. Golden oldies are the songs that resonate in our memories. Merely hearing one triggers a series of related emotions and recollections, which is what makes them golden. Not all songs can be both golden and oldie. *Oldie* means it must have originated in a clearly defined historical past, probably more than ten years ago. The person who hears an oldie on the radio is reminded of the historical time of its origin; thus, the oldie will be suggestive of what was going on culturally. Though that message need not be profound, somehow, in music, style, and lyrics the golden oldie will reveal its context. More important for the individual listener, the golden oldie must have emerged at a key time in his or her life, usually in the adolescent to early adulthood range, a time of acute emotions and restless hormones. Additionally, for an oldie to be truly golden, a poignant response to the song must be shared with others of its host generation. Thus, a song treasured by only two people might be a sentimental favorite, but if it is not sanctioned by the media industry and millions of people, that's all it is. If you are not old enough to cherish a golden oldie, just wait around. Hum, chant, whistle, tap your toe, or shake your booty patiently. You probably have dozens of golden oldies in the making. A few words of warning: Your descendents not yet born may someday scorn the tunes you treasure.

Exercise 2 Discussion and Critical Thinking

Complete the following pattern:

Subject: golden oldie

Principle of Division: components for a definition according to the common use of the term

Parts (components):

1. Historical origin: ten or more years old

2. Revealing of _____

3. Personal _____

4. Must be a shared _____

The Zones of the Sea

Leonard Engel et al.

In this paragraph from The Sea, *published by Time-Life Books, the authors show that the sea can be divided into four zones.*

The life of the ocean is divided into distinct realms, each with its own group of creatures that feed upon each other and depend on each other in different ways. There is, first of all, the tidal zone, where land and sea meet. Then comes the realm of the shallow seas around the continents, which goes down to about 500 feet. It is in these two zones that the vast majority of marine life occurs. The deep ocean adds two regions, the zone of light and the zone of perpetual darkness. In the clear waters of the western Pacific, light could still be seen at a depth of 1,000 feet through the portholes of the *Trieste* on its seven-mile dive.

But for practical purposes the zone of light ends at about 600 feet. Below that level there is too little light to support the growth of the "grass" of the sea—the tiny, single-celled green plants whose ability to form sugar and starch with the aid of sunlight makes them the base of the great food pyramid of the ocean.

Exercise 3   Discussion and Critical Thinking

1. What are the four zones of the sea?

2. Is the paragraph organized by space or by time?

3. What characterizes each zone?

4. Draw a simple cross section of the sea to show the four zones. Make it as elaborate as you like.

✳ Practicing Patterns of Analysis by Division

Exercise 4   Completing Patterns

Fill in the blanks in the following outlines to complete each analysis by division.

1. Unit: Federal government

   Principle: Division of power

   Parts based on the principle:

   I. Executive

   II. _____

   III. _____

2. Unit: Good boss

   Principle: Effectiveness in leading a work force

   Parts based on the principle:

I. Fair

II. _____

III. _____

IV. _____

✳ Topics for Paragraphs of Analysis by Division

Reading-Related Topics

"More Than Ordinary"

1. Write about an ordinary person who has struggled mightily and deserves the title *hero*. Structure your piece around the person's achievements and traits, especially the traits.

2. Write a paragraph of analysis by division about a person who is an excellent role model for you or others you know.

"Golden Oldies"

3. Write a paragraph in which you analyze your favorite golden oldie by discussing its parts, such as when it originated, what it reveals about the culture of that time, and how the oldie touches the lives of others.

"The Zones of the Sea"

4. Using this paragraph as a model, write about the layers of something else, such as skin, bone, a tree, the atmosphere, the earth, or a snow field. Consult an encyclopedia or a textbook for specific information on your topic or for terminology, but be sure to use your own sentences to write the paragraph.

Cross-Curricular Topics

5. Consider the units of material in a class you are taking or have taken. Each unit has its parts: a musical composition in a music-appreciation class, a short story in an English class, an organ such as a heart in a biology class, a government in a political-science class, a management team in a business class, a family in a sociology class, a painting in an art-history class, a teacher or student in an education class, and so on. Select one unit, consult your textbook(s), talk to your instructor(s), and follow the procedure for writing an analysis by division. Credit your sources, and use quotation marks around material you borrow.

Career-Related Topics

6. Explain how the parts of a particular product function as a unit.
7. Explain how each of several qualities of a specific person—intelligence, sincerity, knowledgeability, communication skills, manner, attitude, appearance—makes that individual an effective salesperson, manager, or employee.

General Topics

8. In a paragraph of analysis by division, discuss the qualities that make someone or something successful or praiseworthy. Select one of these subjects:

> A specific performer (a singer, a dancer, an actor, or a musician)
> A team, a company, a school, a class, an organization
> A movie, a television program, a music video, a video game
> A family, a marriage, a relationship, a club

   Begin with a topic sentence such as this (modify it later to make it less mechanical): "_____'s success can be attributed to three [or four] qualities." The qualities would, of course, become the main parts of your outline.
9. Discuss how a physical object works, perhaps a part of the body (heart, ear, lungs), a part of a car (carburetor, water pump), or an object (a CD player, a stapler, a pencil sharpener, a hair dryer).

❋ Writer's Guidelines at a Glance: Analysis by Division

1. Follow the procedure discussed in this chapter from (step 1) unit to (step 2) principle to (step 3) parts to (step 4) discussion.
2. Write a strong topic sentence to unify your writing.
3. Present the parts in a way that promotes order. Consider time, space, and emphasis.
4. Emphasize how the parts function in relation to the operation of the whole unit.
5. Your basic outline will probably look like this:

   I. Part 1
   II. Part 2
   III. Part 3

8

Process Analysis: Writing About Doing

✳ Writing Paragraphs of Process Analysis

If you have any doubt about how frequently we use process analysis, just think about how many times you have heard people say, "How do you do it?" or "How is [was] it done?" Even when you are not hearing those questions, you are posing them yourself when you need to make something, cook a meal, assemble an item, take some medicine, repair your car, or figure out what happened. In your college classes, you may have to discover how osmosis occurs, how a rock changes form, how a mountain was formed, how a battle was won, or how a bill goes through the legislature.

If you need to explain how to do something or how something was (is) done, you will write a paper of **process analysis.** You will break down your topic into stages, explaining each so that your reader can duplicate or understand the process.

Two Types of Process Analysis: Directive and Informative

The questions "How do I do it?" and "How is (was) it done?" will lead you into two different types of process analysis—directive and informative.

Directive process analysis explains how to do something. As the name suggests, it gives directions and gives the reader instructions. It says, for example, "Read me, and you can bake a pie [tune up your car, solve a math problem, write an essay, take some medicine]." Because it is presented directly to the reader, it usually addresses the reader as "you," or it implies the "you" by saying something such as "First [you] purchase a large, fat wombat, and then [you] . . ." In the same way, this textbook addresses you or implies "you" because it is a long how-to-do-it (directive process analysis) statement.

Informative process analysis explains how something was (is) done by giving data (information). Whereas the directive process analysis tells you what to do in the future, the informative process analysis tells you what has occurred or what is occurring. If it is something in nature, such as the formation of a mountain, you can read and understand the process by which it emerged. In this type of process analysis, you do not tell the reader what to do; therefore, you do not use the words *you* or *your*.

Working with Stages

Preparation

In the first stage of writing directive process analysis, list the materials or equipment needed for the process and discuss the necessary setup arrangements. For some topics, this stage will also provide technical terms and definitions. The degree to which this stage is detailed will depend on both the subject itself and the expected knowledge and experience of the projected audience.

Informative process analysis may begin with background or context rather than with preparation. For example, a statement explaining how mountains form might begin with a description of a flat portion of the earth made up of plates that are arranged like a jigsaw puzzle.

Steps

The actual process will be presented here. Each step must be explained clearly and directly, and phrased to accommodate the audience. The language, especially in directive process analysis, is likely to be simple and concise; however, avoid dropping words such as *and, a, an, the,* and *of,* thereby lapsing into "recipe language." In directive process analysis the steps may be accompanied by explanations about why certain procedures are necessary and how not following directions carefully can lead to trouble. In informative process analysis the steps should appear in a logical progression within a sequence.

Order

The order will usually be chronological (time based) in some sense. Certain transitional words are commonly used to promote coherence: *first, second, third, then, soon, now, next, finally, at last, therefore, consequently,* and—especially for informative process analysis—words used to show the passage of time such as hours, days of the week, and so on.

✳ Basic Forms

Consider using this form for directive process analysis (with topics such as how to cook something or how to fix something).

I. Preparation
   A.
   B.
   C.
II. Steps
   A.
   B.
   C.
   D.

Consider using this form for informative process analysis (with topics such as how a volcano functions or how a battle was won).

I. Background or context
   A.
   B.
   C.
II. Change or development (narrative)
   A.
   B.
   C.
   D.

✳ Examining Paragraphs of Process Analysis

Student Writers

Pupusas, Salvadoran Delight

Patty Serrano

We all have at least one kind of food that reminds us of childhood, something that has filled our bellies in times of hunger and perhaps comforted our minds in times of stress. For Patty Serrano, a community college student living at home, that special dish is pupusas. In El Salvador these are a favorite item in homes and restaurants and at roadside stands. In Southern California, they're available in little restaurants called pupusarias.

Every time my mom decides to make pupusas, we jump for joy. A pupusa contains only a few ingredients, and it may sound easy to make, but really good ones must be made by experienced hands. My mom is an expert, having learned as a child from her mother. All the ingredients are chosen fresh. The meat, either pork or beef, can be bought prepared, but my mom chooses to prepare it herself. The meat, which is called "carnitas," is ground and cooked with tomatoes and spices. The cheese-- she uses a white Jalisco--has to be stringy because that kind gives pupusas a very good taste, appearance, and texture. Then comes the preparation of the "masa," or cornmeal. It has to be soft but not so soft that it falls apart in the making and handling. All of this is done while the "comal," or skillet, is being heated. She then grabs a chunk of masa and forms it into a tortilla like a magician turning a ball into a thin pancake. Next she grabs small chunks of meat and cheese and places them in the middle of the tortilla. The tortilla is folded in half and formed again. After placing the pupusa into the sizzling skillet with one hand, she is already starting

another pupusa. It's amazing how she does two
things at the same time. She turns the pupusas
over and over again until she is sure that
they are done. We watch, mouths open, plates
empty. In my family it is a tradition that I
get the first pupusa because I like them so
much. I love opening the hot pupusas, smelling
the aroma, and seeing the stringy cheese
stretching in the middle. I'm as
discriminating as a wine taster. But I never
eat a pupusa without "curtido," chopped
cabbage with jalapeño. Those items balance the
richness of the other ingredients. I could eat
Mom's pupusas forever. I guess it has
something to do with the way my mom makes
them, with experienced, magical, loving hands.

Exercise 1 Discussion and Critical Thinking

1. Underline the topic sentence and the concluding sentences (2).

2. To what kind of audience (well-informed, moderately informed, or poorly informed on the topic) does Serrano direct this selection?

3. What type of process analysis (informative or directive) is used?

4. What is the prevailing tone of this material (objective, humorous, reverent, argumentative, playful, ironic, ridiculing)?

5. Draw a line at the point at which the preparation ends and the steps begin.

6. Use numbers in the margin to indicate the steps in the cooking process.

Making Faces

Seham Hemmat

By evening, Seham Hemmat is a community college student. By day, she is an employee of a mall specialty store where, to use her words, she does "face detail work." She rewrote this paragraph of process analysis six times, twice reading it aloud to her peer group and listening to their suggestions (especially those from the two male members) before she was satisfied with the content and tone. Her word choice suggests a somewhat humorous view of work she takes seriously but not too seriously.

The Face Place, a trendy mall store, is where I work. Making faces is what I do. I don't mean sticking out my tongue; I mean reworking the faces of women who want a new or fresh look. When I get through, if I've done a good job, you can't tell if my subject

Topic sentence is wearing makeup or not. <u>If you'd like to do what I do, just follow these directions.</u>

Imagine you have a client. Her name is Donna.

Preparation <u>Check her out</u> for skin complexion, skin condition, size of eyes, kind of eyebrows, and lip shape. Then <u>go to the supply room and select</u> the <u>items</u> you need for the faceover, including a cleanser and toner with added

Steps moisturizers. <u>Put them on a tray by your</u>

brushes and other tools and basic supplies.

1 Begin by stripping off her old makeup with a
few cotton balls and cleanser. Donna's skin
is a combination of conditions. Her forehead,
nose, and chin are oily, and her cheeks are

2 dry. Scrub her down with Tea Tree, my
favorite facial cleanser from a product line
that is not tested on animals. Scour the oil

3 slicks extra. Then slather on some Tea Tree
toner to close her pores so the dirt doesn't

4 go back in. Add a very light moisturizer such
as one called Elderflower Gel. Donna has a

5 pale complexion. Put on a coat of 01
foundation, the fairest in the shop, which
evens out her skin tone. Next, with a big

6 face brush, dust on a layer of 01 powder to
give her a smooth, dry look. Now Donna, who's
watching in a mirror, speaks up to say she
wants her eyebrows brushed and lightened just
a bit. She has dark eyebrows and eyelashes
that won't require much mascara or eyebrow

7 pencil. So use gel to fix the eyebrows in
place while you trim, shape, and pencil them.
Move downward on the face, going next to her

8 eyes. Use brown mascara to curl her already

9 dark lashes. With your blusher brush, dab

10 some peach rose blush on her cheeks and blend
it in. Line her lips with bronze sand lip

liner pencil and <u>fill in the rest</u> with rouge

mauve lipstick. Swing Donna around to the big

lighted mirror. Watch her pucker her lips,

squint her eyes, flirt with herself. See her

smile. Now you pocket the tip. Feel good.

Concluding <u>You've just given a woman a new face, and</u>
sentence
<u>she's out to conquer the world.</u>

Exercise 2   Discussion and Critical Thinking

1. Is this paragraph of process analysis mainly directive or informative?

2. How does Hemmat take her paragraph beyond a list of mechanical directions?

3. In addition to using chronological order (time), what other order does she use briefly?

4. What word choice may have come from suggestions offered by the males in her discussion group?

Professional Writers

The Birth of an Island

Rachel Carson

> *We usually think of birth in a biological sense, but Rachel Carson describes a different kind—a geological birth. It requires no coach, no midwife, no obstetrician. And unless you can live for thousands or even millions of years, you can't witness the whole process. Nevertheless, it is a process, and it can be described in steps.*

The birth of a volcanic island is an event marked by prolonged and violent travail: the forces of the earth striving to create, and all the forces of the sea opposing. The sea floor, where an island begins, is probably nowhere more than about fifty miles thick—a thin covering over the vast bulk of the earth. In it are deep cracks and fissures, the results of unequal cooling and shrinkage in past ages. Along such lines of weakness the molten lava from the earth's interior presses up and finally bursts forth into the sea. But a submarine volcano is different from a terrestrial eruption, where lava, molten rocks, gases, and other ejecta are hurled into the air through an open crater. Here on the bottom of the ocean the volcano has been resisting all the weight of the ocean water above it. Despite the immense pressure of, it may be, two or three miles of sea water, the new volcanic cone builds upward toward the surface in flow after flow of lava. Once within reach of the waves, its soft ash and tuff are violently attacked, and for a long period the potential island may remain a shoal, unable to emerge. But, eventually, in new eruptions, the cone is pushed up into the air and a rampart against the attacks of the waves is built of hardened lava.

Exercise 3   Discussion and Critical Thinking

1. What type of process analysis (informative or directive) is used?

2. For what type of audience (well informed, moderately informed, or poorly informed on the topic) is Carson writing?

3. Underline four transitional terms used in this paragraph.

How to Sharpen a Knife

Florence H. Pettit

> *The simplest tasks are often the most poorly done because we assume that we know how to do them and do not seek instruction. Florence H. Pettit explains here how to sharpen a knife properly, and what we learn reminds us that we could probably take lessons on performing any number of everyday chores.*

If you have never done any whittling or wood carving before, the first skill to learn is how to sharpen your knife. You may be surprised to learn that even a brand-new knife needs sharpening. Knives are never sold honed (finely sharpened), although some gouges and chisels are. It is essential to learn the firm stroke on the stone that will keep your blades sharp. The sharpening stone must be fixed in place on the table, so that it will not move around. You can do this by placing a rubber inner tube or a thin piece of foam rubber under it. Or you can tack four strips of wood, if you have a rough worktable, to frame the stone and hold it in place. Put a generous puddle of oil on the stone—this will soon disappear into the surface of a new stone, and you will need to keep adding more oil. Press the knife blade flat against the stone in the puddle of oil, using your index finger. Whichever way the cutting edge of the knife faces is the side of the blade that should get a little more pressure. Move the blade around three or four times in a narrow oval about the size of your fingernail, going *counterclockwise* when the sharp edge is facing right. Now turn the blade over in the same spot on the stone, press hard, and move it around the small oval *clockwise,* with more pressure on the cutting edge that faces left. Repeat the ovals, flipping the knife blade over six or seven times, and applying lighter pressure to the blade the last two times. Wipe the blade clean with a piece of rag or tissue and rub it flat on the piece of leather strop at least twice on each side. Stroke *away* from the cutting edge to remove the little burr of metal that may be left on the blade.

Exercise 4 Discussion and Critical Thinking

1. What type of process analysis (informative or directive) is used?

2. To what type of audience (well informed, moderately informed, or poorly informed on the topic) does Pettit direct this selection?

3. What is the prevailing tone (objective, humorous, reverent, argumentative, cautionary, playful, ironic, ridiculing) of this selection?

4. Make an X at the point at which the preparation (materials, setup, explaining words, and so on) ends and the steps begin.

5. Write numbers in the margin to indicate the steps or stages in the process.

6. Circle any transitional words indicating time or other progression (*first, second, then, soon, now, next, after, before, when, finally, at last, therefore, consequently,* and—especially for the informative process analysis—words used to show the passage of time, such as hours, days of the week, and so on).

7. Is Pettit trying to inform or to persuade?

✳ **Practicing Patterns of Processs Analysis**

Exercise 5 Completing a Directive Pattern

Refer to the paragraph on pages 94–95. Fill in the blanks in the following outline to complete the process analysis; the analysis is informative but can be taken as directive (as it appears here).

"*Pupusas,* Salvadoran Delight"

  I. Preparation

    A. Ingredients fresh

    B. Meat—either beef or pork

 II. Steps

    A. _____

    B. _____

    C. _____

    D. _____

    E. _____

    F. _____

    G. _____

Exercise 6   Completing an Informative Pattern

Refer to the paragraph on page 98–99. Fill in the blanks in the following outline to complete the informative process analysis.

"The Birth of an Island"

I. Background or context

   A. Sea floor

   B. Cracks in surface

II. Change or development

   A. _____

   B. Cone builds toward surface

   C. _____

   D. _____

✳ Topics for Paragraphs of Process Analysis

Reading-Related Topics

"*Pupusas:* Salvadoran Delight"

1. Write about a special food prepared in your family now or in your childhood. The food could be your favorite dish, or it might be a treat prepared for a holiday.

"Making Faces"

2. Using this paragraph as a model (omit the hypothetical customer if you like), write about any other grooming or personal service that you either perform for hire or understand very well and can perform. Suggestions include hair styling, manicures, pedicures, facials, tattooing or painting skin, and skin alteration (piercing).

"The Birth of an Island"

3. Using this paragraph as a guide, write about the formation of something else in nature. You could write about a geographical feature such as an alluvial plain, a beach, a lake, a mountain, a desert, or a delta. Or you could write about something from the

field of chemistry, biology, or astronomy. For specific information or terminology, refer to general sources such as encyclopedias or introductory textbooks, but be sure to use your own sentences to write the paragraph.

"How to Sharpen a Knife"

4. Use this selection as a model to explain how to perform another simple task such as cleaning a shower or an oven, snow-sealing boots, defrosting a refrigerator, or waxing a car.

Cross-Curricular Topics

5. Write a paragraph about a procedure you follow in your college work in a science (chemistry, biology, geology) lab. You may explain how to analyze a rock, how to dissect something, how to operate something, how to perform an experiment.
6. Write a paragraph about how to do something in an activity or performance class, such as drama, physical education, art, or music.

Career-Related Topics

7. Explain how to display, package, sell, or demonstrate a product.
8. Explain how to perform a service or how to repair or install a product.
9. Explain the procedure for operating a machine, a computer, a piece of equipment, or another device.
10. Explain how to manufacture, construct, or cook something.

General Topics

Most of the following topics are directive as they are phrased. However, each can be transformed into a how-it-was-done informative topic by personalizing it and explaining stage by stage how you, someone else, or a group did something. For example, you could write either a directive process analysis about how to deal with an obnoxious person or an informative process analysis about how you or someone else dealt with an obnoxious person. Keep in mind that the two types of process analysis are often blended, especially in the personal approach. Many of the following topics will be more interesting to you and your readers if they are personalized.

Select one of the following topics and write a process-analysis paragraph about it. Most of the topics require some narrowing to be treated in a paragraph. For example, writing about playing baseball is too broad; writing about how to throw a curve ball may be manageable.

11. How to end a relationship without hurting someone's feelings

12. How to pass a test for a driver's license

13. How to get a job at _____

14. How to eat _____

15. How to perform a magic trick

16. How to repair _____

17. How to assemble _____

18. How to learn about another culture

19. How to approach someone you would like to know better

✳ Writer's Guidelines at a Glance: Process Analysis

1. Decide whether your process analysis is mainly directive or informative, and be appropriately consistent in using pronouns and other designations:

   ▪ For the **directive analysis,** use the second person, addressing the reader as *you*. The *you* may be understood, even if it is not written.

   ▪ For the **informative analysis,** use

   a. the first person, speaking as *I* or *we*, or
   b. the third person, speaking about the subject as *he, she, it,* or *they*, or by name.

2. Consider using these basic forms.

Directive	Informative
I. Preparation	I. Background or context
A.	A.
B.	B.
II. Steps	II. Change or development
A.	A.
B.	B.
C.	C.

3. In explaining the stages and using technical terms, take into account whether your audience will be mainly well informed, moderately informed, or poorly informed.

4. Use transitional words indicating time or other progression (such as *first, second, then, soon, now, next, after, before, when, finally, at last, therefore, consequently,* and—especially for the informative process analysis—words that show passage of time, such as hours, days of the week, and so on).

5. Avoid "recipe language" by not dropping *the, a, an,* or *of.*

9

Cause and Effect: Determining Reasons and Outcomes

✳ Writing Paragraphs of Cause and Effect

Cause-and-effect relationships are common in our daily lives. A single situation may raise questions about both causes and effects:

> *The car won't start.*
>
> *Why?* (cause)
>
> *What now?* (effect)

In a paragraph, you will probably concentrate on either causes or effects, although you may mention both of them. Because you cannot write about all causes or all effects, you should try to identify and develop the most important ones. Consider that some causes are immediate, others remote; some visible, others hidden. Any one or a group of causes can be the most important. The effects of an event can also be complicated. Some may be immediate, others long-range. The sequence of events is not necessarily related to causation. For example, *B* (inflation) may follow *A* (the election of a president), but that sequence does not mean that *A* caused *B*.

Organizing Cause and Effect

One useful approach to developing a cause-and-effect analysis is **listing.** Write down the event, situation, or trend you are concerned about. Then, on the left side of the page list the causes and on the right side list the effects. Looking at the two lists, determine the best side (causes or effects) for your study.

Causes	Event, Situation, or Trend	Effects
Bad habits In-law problems Religious differences Career decision Personal abuse Infidelity Sexual incompatibility Politics Money	*Divorce*	Financial problems Liberation Financial success Safety New relationships Social adjustment Vocational choice Problems for children Independence

First, evaluate the items on your list. Keep in mind that one cause, such as personal abuse, may have its own (remote, hidden, or underlying) cause or partial cause: frustration over job loss, mental problems, drug addiction, bad parenting, or weak character. In single paragraphs, one usually deals with immediate causes, such as in-law problems, money, and personal abuse. (These same principles can be applied to effects.)

After you have evaluated the items on your list, choose two or three of the most important causes or effects and proceed.

The causes could be incorporated into a preliminary topic sentence and then developed in an outline.

Topic sentence: The main causes of my divorce were in-law problems, money, and personal abuse.

I. In-law problems
   A. Helped too much
   B. Expected too much
II. Money
   A. Poor management
   B. Low-paying job
III. Personal abuse
   A. Verbal
   B. Physical

Your paragraph will derive its structure from either causes or effects, although both causes and effects may be mentioned.

Give emphasis and continuity to your writing by repeating key words, such as *cause, reason, effect, result, consequence,* and *outcome.*
  The basic structure of your paragraph will look like this:

Topic sentence
Cause (or Effect) 1
Cause (or Effect) 2
Cause (or Effect) 3

✳ Examining Paragraphs of Cause and Effect

Student Writers

A Divorce with Reasons

Sarah Bailey

A few years have passed, and student Sarah Bailey can look back on her divorce and sort out the causes and effects of her failed marriage. This paragraph, which focuses on three main causes, was developed through the listing and outlining shown on page 107.

I was married for almost five years. The first year was great, but each of the last four was worse than the previous one. The marriage was made in carefree leisure, and the divorce was made in a reality that just got colder and colder. Our first problem was the in-laws, actually his parents; mine live in another state, and we saw them only once a year. It was nothing deliberate. His parents wanted to help, and that was the problem. They expected me to be the daughter they never had and him to be a successful businessman and homeowner. They expected too much from both of us, and we couldn't make our own choices. That cause was related to another one--money. Both of us had low-level jobs in industry. We were around people who were wealthy, but we couldn't buy, belong, and participate as we wanted to. Then I started getting more promotions than he. Finally, he quit his job just at the beginning of a recession, and he couldn't get another one. I told him I would be patient, but at times I was resentful that I was the only one working. As he became more and more frustrated, he started losing his temper with me and said things that hurt my feelings. One day he hit me. He said he was sorry and even cried, but I could not forgive him. We got a divorce. It took me a while before I could look back and see what the causes really were, but by then it was too late to make any changes.

Exercise 1   Discussion and Critical Thinking

1. Underline the topic sentence and the concluding sentence.

2. What were the three main causes of the failed marriage?

3. Bailey says it took her too long to discover the causes, so she
   was unable to deal with the problems. Looking at this case in
   speculation, would you say the problems can be found mainly in
   character or circumstance? Explain.

More Than the Classroom

Richard Blaylock

*Responding to an assignment on a topic organized mainly around
causes and effects, Richard Blaylock chose to write about the consequences of his becoming a college student. With much trepida-
tion, at thirty-three he had enrolled in the evening program at a
local community college. The reasons for his being there were
multiple, and so, surprising to him, were the results.*

"We think you would benefit from our
work-study program," he said to me. He wasn't
my high school counselor, and I wasn't 18. He
was the division manager, and he had just
offered to pay my expenses for attending a
local community college. At 33, I was working
for a large company in a dead-end job, dead-
end because I wasn't qualified for any
management positions. Naturally, I enrolled in
college. More benefits than I expected were to
follow. I had hardly started when the first
response greeted me: my family was clearly
proud. I heard my two kids in elementary
school bragging about me to kids in the
neighborhood. They even brought me some of
their tough homework questions. My wife had

lots of questions about college. We talked
about taking a class together. Unlike me, she
had been a good student in high school. Then I
had had no interest in going on to college.
Now I did, and one thing led to another.
A geography class connected me with a geology
class. A political science class moved me to
subscribe to the *Los Angeles Times*. I became
more curious about a variety of subjects, and
I felt more confident in dealing with ideas.
At work my supervisors started asking me to
become more involved in ongoing projects and
planning. By the time I had taken my second
English class, I was writing reports with
much more confidence and skill. Now, after
receiving a good job review and being
interviewed by my plant manager, I am in line
for a promotion that I once thought was
beyond my reach. I had expected mainly a
classroom. I found much more.

Exercise 2 Discussion and Critical Thinking

1. Is this a paragraph mainly of causes or effects?

2. Circle the topic sentence.

3. Underline each effect.

Professional Writers

Results of Underage Drinking

Wayne D. Hoyer and Deborah J. MacInnis

> *In their college textbook* Consumer Behavior, *Professors Wayne D. Hoyer and Deborah J. MacInnis discuss the perils of underage drinking as a major problem for both the individual drinkers and society.*

Nearly 45 percent of college students have engaged in "binge drinking" (consuming more than five drinks in one sitting). Four million minors are alcoholics or problem drinkers. This often-downplayed behavior has a devastating impact on both themselves and society at large. Overuse of alcohol has been involved in 70 percent of campus violence cases, 68 percent of campus property damage cases, and 40 percent of academic failures, making it the primary discipline, emotional, and physical problem on college campuses. Alcohol is also involved in roughly half of teen highway fatalities, half of all youth suicides, and 90 percent of campus hazing deaths. Almost half of all schools polled say alcohol is the most serious problem they face. Alcohol is implicated even in the rising costs of college tuition. Now that colleges are liable for campus drinking incidents, the cost of insurance (and hence tuition) has skyrocketed. Accidents due to drinking also contribute to the high cost of automobile insurance for young consumers. To combat these problems, groups like Mothers Against Drunk Driving (MADD) and Students Against Drunk Driving (SADD) work to enact legislation to punish drinking and driving, use social disapproval to pressure students not to drink and drive, and institute programs that stress the importance of having a designated driver.

Exercise 3   Discussion and Critical Thinking

1. Circle the topic sentence.

2. Underline the concluding sentence that completes the developed idea. *Hint:* The topic sentence states the problem, the

development gives support for that view, and the concluding sentence gives a final response to the topic sentence.

3. Is this paragraph organized around mainly causes or effects?

4. Complete the following list to show the main effects. Add additional points if you like.

> Topic Sentence: Underage drinking has devastating effects on both the consumer and society at large.
>
> 1. Campus violence
> 2. Campus _____
> 3. Academic _____
> 4. Teen highway fatalities
> 5. Youth suicides
> 6. Campus _____
> 7. Rising _____
> 8. High cost of _____

5. Why are problems caused by the use of other drugs discussed more than those caused by the use of alcohol?

6. Which of these effects pertain more to four-year colleges with mostly resident students than to colleges with mostly commuter students?

✳ Practicing Patterns of Cause and Effect

Exercise 4 Completing Patterns

Fill in the blanks in the following outlines to complete first the causes outline and then the effects outline.

1. Causes for immigrating to the United States

    I. Desire for a better education

    II. _____

    III. _____

    IV. _____

2. Effects of getting adequate exercise

    I. Muscle tone

    II. _____

    III. _____

    IV. _____

✳ Topics for Paragraphs of Cause and Effect

Reading-Related Topics

"A Divorce with Reasons"

1. Write a paragraph about the effects of a divorce on someone you know, either a divorced person or a relative of a divorced person.
2. Write about the causes for or effects of the good marriage of a couple you know.

"More Than the Classroom"

3. Using this paragraph as a model, write a paragraph about the causes and effects of any new element in your life at any point. The element could be a relationship, death, health problem, marriage, college program, new job, or winning ticket in the lottery.

"Results of Underage Drinking"

4. Pick three effects of underage drinking from this paragraph and discuss them in relation to what you have specifically observed.
5. Using this paragraph as a model, write about the causes of underage drinking and conclude with a brief statement about what can be done to counteract those causes.

Cross-Curricular Topics

6. From a class that you are taking or have taken, select a subject that is especially concerned with causes and effects and develop a topic. Begin by selecting an event, a situation, or a trend in the class content and make a list of the causes or effects; that procedure will almost immediately show you whether you have a topic you can discuss effectively. Class notes and textbooks can provide you with more specific information. If you use textbooks or other materials, give credit to the sources. Instructors across the campus may have suggestions for studies of cause and effect. Some areas for your search include history, political science, geology, astronomy, psychology, philosophy, sociology, real estate, child development, education, fashion merchandising, psychiatric technician program, nursing, police science, fire science, physical education, and restaurant and food-service management.

Career-Related Topics

7. Discuss the effects (benefits) of a particular product or service on the business community, family life, society generally, specific groups (age, income, activities), or an individual.
8. Discuss the needs (thus the cause of development) by individuals, families, or institutions for a particular product or type of product.
9. Discuss the effects of using a certain approach, system, or philosophy in sales, human resources, or customer service.

General Topics

10. Write a paragraph about the causes of crime (for one individual involved in crime), unemployment (one person who is out of work), leaving home (one person who has left home), emigrating (one person or family), poverty (one person who is poor), school dropout (one person), going to college (one who did), or the success of a product or program on television (one).
11. Write a paragraph about the effects of disease (a particular disease, perhaps on just one person), fighting (one or two people involved in a dispute), fire (a particular one), alcoholism (a certain alcoholic), getting a job (a person with a particular job), early marriage (a person who married very young), teenage parenthood (one person or a couple), or dressing a certain way (one person and his or her style).

✳ Writer's Guidelines at a Glance: Cause and Effect

1. Have your purpose clearly in mind.
2. Be sure that you have sufficient knowledge of the subject to develop it.
3. Distinguish clearly between causes and effects by using three columns. From your lists select only the most relevant causes or effects.

Causes	Event, Situation, or Trend	Effects

4. Concentrate primarily on either causes or effects. You may refer to both causes and effects, but use only one as the framework for writing your paragraph.
5. Do not conclude that something is an effect merely because it follows something else.
6. Emphasize your main concern, cause or effect, by repeating key words such as *cause, reason, effect, result, consequence,* and *outcome.*

10

Classification: Establishing Groups

※ Writing Paragraphs of Classification

To explain by classification, you put persons, places, things, or ideas into groups, or classes, based on their characteristics. Whereas analysis by division deals with the characteristics of just one unit, classification deals with more than one unit, so the subject is plural.

To classify efficiently, try following this procedure:

1. Select a plural subject.
2. Decide on a principle for grouping the units of the subject.
3. Establish the groups, or classes.
4. Write about the classes.

Selecting a Subject

When you say you have different kinds of neighbors, friends, teachers, bosses, or interests, you are classifying; that is, you are forming groups.

In naming the different kinds of people in your neighborhood, you might think of different groupings of your neighbors, the units. For example, some neighbors are friendly, some are meddlesome, and some are private. Some neighbors have yards like Japanese gardens, some have yards like neat but cozy parks, and some have yards like abandoned lots. Some neighbors are affluent, some are comfortable, and some are struggling. Each of these sets is a classification system and could be the focus of a paragraph.

Using a Principle to Avoid Overlapping

All the sets in the preceding section are sound because each group is based on a single concern: neighborly involvement, appearance of the yard, or wealth. This one concern, or controlling idea, is called the **principle.** For example, the principle of neighborly involvement controls the grouping of neighbors into three classes: friendly, meddlesome, and private.

All the classes in any one group must adhere to the controlling principle for that group. You would not say, for example, that your neighbors can be classified as friendly, meddlesome, private, and affluent, because the first three classes relate to neighborly involvement, but the fourth, relating to wealth, refers to another principle. Any one of the first three—the friendly, meddlesome, and private—might also be affluent. The classes should not overlap in this way. Also, every member should fit into one of the available classes.

Establishing Classes

As you name your classes, rule out easy, unimaginative phrasing such as *fast/medium/slow, good/average/bad,* and *beautiful/ordinary/ugly.* Look for creative, original phrases and unusual perspectives.

> *Subject:* neighbors
> *Principle:* neighborhood involvement
> *Classes:* friendly, meddlesome, private

> *Subject:* neighbors
> *Principle:* yard upkeep
> *Classes:* immaculate, neat, messy

> *Subject:* neighbors
> *Principle:* wealth
> *Classes:* affluent, comfortable, struggling

Using Simple and Complex Forms

Classification can take two forms: simple and complex. The simple form does not go beyond main divisions in its groupings.

> *Subject:* Neighbors
> *Principle:* Involvement
> *Classes:*   I. Friendly
>   II. Meddlesome
>   III. Private

Complex classifications are based on one principle and then are subgrouped by another related principle. The following example classifies neighbors by their neighborly involvement. It then subgroups two of the classes on the basis of motive.

I. Friendly
II. Meddlesome
   A. Controlling
   B. Emotionally needy
III. Private
   A. Shy
   B. Snobbish
   C. Secretive

Exercise 1 Avoiding Overlapped Classes

Mark each set of classes as correct (OK) or overlapping (OL); circle the classes that overlap.

	Subject	Principle	Classes
Example: OL	community college students	intentions	vocational academic transfer specialty needs (hardworking)
_____ 1.	airline flights	passenger seating	first class business coach
_____ 2.	country singers	clothing trademark	hat overalls decorative costume expensive
_____ 3.	schools	ownership	private religious public
_____ 4.	faces	shape	round square oval beautiful broad long
_____ 5.	dates	behavior resembling aquatic animals	sharks clams jellyfish cute octopuses

✳ Examining Paragraphs of Classification

Student Writer

Doctors Have Their Symptoms Too

Boris Belinsky

*Drawing on his own experiences and those of his family, student
Boris Belinsky groups doctors according to their motives.*

<table>
<tr>
<td></td>
<td>Because I come from a large family that</td>
</tr>
<tr>
<td></td>
<td>unfortunately has had a lot of illnesses, I</td>
</tr>
<tr>
<td></td>
<td>have learned to classify doctors according to</td>
</tr>
<tr>
<td>Topic
sentence</td>
<td>why they became doctors. <u>As doctors can</u></td>
</tr>
<tr>
<td></td>
<td><u>diagnose illnesses by the symptoms they</u></td>
</tr>
<tr>
<td></td>
<td><u>identify, I can figure out doctors' motives</u></td>
</tr>
<tr>
<td></td>
<td><u>by their symptoms, by which I mean behavior.</u></td>
</tr>
<tr>
<td></td>
<td>Some doctors have chosen the field of</td>
</tr>
<tr>
<td>Support
(class)</td>
<td>medicine because they want to make <u>money</u>.</td>
</tr>
<tr>
<td></td>
<td>They hurry their patients (customers) through</td>
</tr>
<tr>
<td></td>
<td>their multiple office spaces, answering few</td>
</tr>
<tr>
<td></td>
<td>questions, and never sitting down. Although</td>
</tr>
<tr>
<td></td>
<td>slow to answer the desperate phone calls,</td>
</tr>
<tr>
<td></td>
<td>they're fast with the bills. The second class</td>
</tr>
<tr>
<td>Support
(class)</td>
<td>is the group with <u>scientific</u> interests. Not</td>
</tr>
<tr>
<td></td>
<td>as much concerned about money, they're often</td>
</tr>
<tr>
<td></td>
<td>found in university hospitals where they</td>
</tr>
<tr>
<td></td>
<td>teach and work on special medical problems.</td>
</tr>
<tr>
<td></td>
<td>They may be a bit remote and explain symptoms</td>
</tr>
<tr>
<td></td>
<td>in technical terms. The third group is my</td>
</tr>
<tr>
<td>Support
(class)</td>
<td>favorite: those who became doctors to <u>help</u></td>
</tr>
<tr>
<td></td>
<td><u>people</u>. They spend much time with patients,</td>
</tr>
</table>

```
                 often practice in areas that are not
                 affluent, advocate preventative methods,
Concluding       and do volunteer work. Not all doctors
sentence
                 easily fall into these three groups, but
                 virtually every one has a tendency to do so.
```

Exercise 2 Discussion and Critical Thinking

1. What is the principle on which Belinsky's classification is based?

2. How does Belinsky protect himself against a charge that some doctors are not easily classified?

3. Why has Belinsky had occasion to make the observations on which this paragraph is based?

Professional Writers

Behavioral, Psychological, and Medical Effects of Workplace Stress

Gregory Moorhead and Ricky W. Griffin

Stress at the workplace, like cholesterol, can be either good or bad. In this adaptation from Organizational Behavior *by Professors Gregory Moorhead and Ricky W. Griffin, bad stress effects on the individual are grouped in a comprehensive set of classes.*

Stress at the workplace can have a number of consequences for individuals. Under some conditions, stress can be positive, producing desirable energy, enthusiasm, and motivation. But of more concern are the negative results of stress, which can be classified as behavioral, psychological, and medical. The behavioral consequences of stress may certainly harm the persons experiencing the stress, and it may even harm others indirectly. One such behavior is smoking. Research has clearly documented that people who smoke tend to smoke more when they are under stress. There is also evidence that alcohol and drug abuse are often linked to stress. Other possible behavioral consequences are accident proneness, violence, and eating disorders. The second type of stress-induced problems is psychological. When people experience too much stress at work, they may become depressed or find themselves sleeping too much or not enough. Stress may also lead to family dysfunction and sexual difficulties. Often intertwined with these adverse psychological effects is a third category: medical problems. Heart disease and stroke, among other illnesses, have been linked to stress. Other common medical problems as a result of too much stress include headaches, backaches, ulcers, stomach and intestinal disorders, and skin conditions such as acne and hives. Organizations that employ these stressed individuals also may suffer, but it is the individuals who pay the real price.

Exercise 3   Discussion and Critical Thinking

1. Circle the topic sentence.

2. Underline the concluding sentence.

3. Complete this simple outline.

> Topic sentence: Negative results of stress can be grouped into three classes.

>   I. Behavioral
> II. _____
> III. _____

4. Can the same stress produce opposite effects on two people? Give an example.

5. How are the three classes of stress organized—from the most important to the least important or from the least important to the most important?

6. What other pattern of organization is used extensively in this paragraph?

Styles of Leadership

William M. Pride, Robert J. Hughes, and Jack R. Kapoor

Written by three business professors, this paragraph is excerpted from a college textbook. It refers mainly to business institutions and the workplace, but it also covers all social units that depend on leadership, from the family to nations.

For many years, leadership was viewed as a combination of personality traits, such as self-confidence, concern for people, intelligence, and dependability. Achieving a consensus on which traits were most important was difficult, however, and attention turned to styles of leadership behavior. In the last few decades, several styles of leadership have been identified: authoritarian, laissez-faire, and democratic. The **authoritarian leader** holds all authority and responsibility, with communication usually moving from top to bottom. This leader assigns workers to specific tasks and expects orderly, precise results. The leaders at United Parcel Service employ authoritarian leadership. At the other extreme is the **laissez-faire leader,** who gives authority to employees. With the laissez-faire style, subordinates are allowed to work as they choose with a minimum of interference. Communication flows horizontally among group members. Leaders at Apple Computer are known to employ a laissez-faire leadership style in order to give employees as much freedom as possible to develop new products. The **democratic leader** holds final responsibility but also delegates authority to others, who participate in determining work assignments. In this leadership style, communication is active both upward and downward. Employee commitment is high because of participation in the decision-making process. Managers for both Wal-Mart and Saturn have used the democratic leadership style to encourage employees to become more than just rank-and-file workers.

Exercise 4 Discussion and Critical Thinking

1. Underline the topic sentence.

2. What is the subject of this paragraph?

3. What is the principle that divides the subject into classes?

4. This paragraph is obviously concerned with explaining the different styles of leadership, without showing favor. Do you have a preference? If so, what is your preference and why?

5. In the textbook *Business*, Seventh Edition, this paragraph is followed by another with this first sentence: "Today most management experts agree that no one 'best' managerial leadership style exists." How do you think the authors explain such a statement?

✳ Practicing Patterns of Classification

Exercise 5   Completing Patterns

Fill in the blanks in the following outlines to identify classes that could be discussed for each subject.

1. *Subject:* community college students
   Principle: why they attend college
   Classes:

   I. Specialty needs (to take specific courses)

   II. _____

   III. _____

2. *Subject:* romantic dates
   Principle: characterized by behavior similar to that of aquatic animals
   Classes:

   I. Sharks

   II. _____

   III. _____

   IV. _____

❋ Topics for Paragraphs of Classification

Reading-Related Topics

"Doctors Have Their Symptoms Too"

1. Classify another vocational group (clergy, teachers, lawyers, police officers, shop owners) according to their reasons for selecting their field.

"Behavioral, Psychological, and Medical Effects of Workplace Stress"

2. Using this paragraph as a model, write about a workplace or other organization that was damaged by stress (perhaps bad management, unrealistic requirements, or unpleasant coworkers). Your classes might be these groups of negative effects, meaning how things got worse:

   I. Working conditions (including prevailing attitudes, feelings about working there)
   II. Financial (profit for the organization, need not be specific)
   III. Efficiency (for delivering products and/or services with high quality and in sufficient quantity)

With a bit of modification this pattern could be applied to a school (even a classroom) or a family.

"Styles of Leadership"

3. Using the basic definition of leadership by Pride, Hughes, and Kapoor, write a longer piece in which you use at least one example from your experience to explain each class.
4. Write about these classes of leadership as they apply to leading outside the workplace. Consider family, sports, politics, and religion for another area where leadership is important. You may want to argue that one style is better in a situation you define.

Cross-Curricular Topics

5. Write a paragraph on one of the following terms.

   - Business: Types of real-estate sales, banking, management styles, interviews, evaluations.
   - Geology: Types of rocks, earthquakes, mountains, rivers, erosion, faults.

- Biology: Types of cells, viruses, proteins, plants (working mainly with subgroups).
- Psychology: Types of stressors, aggression, adjustments, love.
- Sociology: Types of families, parents, deviants.
- Music: Types of instruments, singers, symphonies, operas, folk songs, rock, rap.

Career-Related Topics

6. Discuss the different types of managers you have encountered (democratic, authoritarian, authoritative, autocratic, buddylike, aloof).
7. Discuss the different types of customers with whom you have dealt (perhaps according to their purpose for seeking your services or products).
8. Discuss the different types of employees you have observed.
9. Discuss the different qualities of products or services in a particular field.

General Topics

Select one of the following groups and decide on a principle for classifying the members. For example, *laughs* might be grouped according to reasons for laughing.

10. Summer jobs
11. Houses
12. Parks
13. Neighborhoods
14. Motorcycles
15. Pet owners
16. Home computers
17. Churchgoers
18. Laughs
19. TV watchers
20. Parties
21. Mail
22. Music

✳ Writer's Guidelines at a Glance: Classification

1. Follow this procedure for writing paragraphs of classification:

   - Select a plural subject.
   - Decide on a principle for grouping the units of the subject.
   - Establish the classes (groups).
   - Write about the classes.

2. Avoid uninteresting phrases for your classes, such as *good/average/bad, fast/medium/slow,* and *beautiful/ordinary/ugly.*
3. Avoid overlapping classes.
4. Use the writing process to help you arrange your material systematically.
5. Use Roman-numeral headings to indicate classes.

   I. Class one
   II. Class two
   III. Class three

6. If you use subclasses, clearly indicate the different levels.
7. Following your outline, give somewhat equal (whatever is appropriate) space to each class.

✳ 11

Comparison and Contrast: Showing Similarities and Differences

✳ Writing Paragraphs of Comparison and Contrast

Comparison and contrast is a method of showing similarities and dissimilarities between subjects. Comparison is concerned with organizing and developing points of similarity; contrast has the same function for dissimilarity. Sometimes a writing assignment may require that you cover only similarities or only dissimilarities. Occasionally, an instructor may ask you to separate one from the other. Usually, you will combine them in a paragraph. For convenience, the term *comparison* is often applied to both comparison and contrast, because both use the same techniques and are usually combined into one operation.

Generating Topics and Working with the 4 *P*'s

Comparison and contrast is basic to your thinking. In your daily activities, you consider similarities and dissimilarities among persons, things, concepts, political leaders, doctors, friends, instructors, schools, nations, classes, movies, and so on. You naturally turn to comparison and contrast to solve problems and to make decisions in your affairs and in your writing. Because you have had so many comparative experiences, finding a topic to write about is likely to be only a matter of choosing from a great number of appealing ideas. Freewriting, brainstorming, and clustering will help you generate topics that are especially workable and appropriate for particular assignments.

Many college writing assignments will specify a topic or ask you to choose one from a list. Regardless of the source of your topic, the procedure for developing your ideas by comparison and contrast is the same as the procedure for developing topics of your own choosing. That procedure can be appropriately called the "4 P's": *purpose, points, patterns,* and *presentation.*

Purpose

Are you trying to show relationships (how things are similar and dissimilar) or to show that one side is better (ranking)? If you want to show that one actor, one movie, one writer, one president, one product, or one idea is better than another, your purpose is to persuade. You will emphasize the superiority of one side over the other in your topic sentence and in your support.

If you want to explain something about a topic by showing each subject in relation to others, then your purpose is informative. For example, you might be comparing two composers, Beethoven and Mozart. Both were musical geniuses, so you then decide it would be senseless to argue that one is superior to the other. Instead, you choose to reveal interesting information about both by showing them in relation to each other.

You may have heard people talk about puppy love and true love and now you decide to explore those two varieties as a topic for a comparative study. Your purpose would be to explain that puppy love and true love are different.

Points

Continuing with the example of two types of love, you would come up with a list of ideas, or points, that you could apply somewhat equally to the two types. From the list, you would select two or three and circle them.

(passion)
(intimacy)
age of lovers
(commitment)
duration
circumstances

Patterns

You then would need to organize your material according to the two basic patterns: subject by subject and point by point. The **subject-by-subject pattern** presents all of one side and then all of the other side.

   I. Puppy love
      A. Passion
      B. Intimacy
      C. Commitment
  II. True love
      A. Passion
      B. Intimacy
      C. Commitment

The **point-by-point pattern** shows the points in relation to the sides (subjects) one at a time. This is the more common pattern.

    I. Passion
      A. Puppy love
        1. Consuming
        2. Intense
      B. True love
        1. Present
        2. Proportional
   II. Intimacy
      A. Puppy love
        1. Lots of talking
        2. Superficial
      B. True love
        1. Good communication
          a. Feelings
          b. Ideas
        2. Deep
III. Commitment
      A. Puppy love
        1. Not tested
        2. Weak, if at all
      B. True love
        1. Proven
        2. Profound

Presentation

Here you would use your outline (or cluster list) to begin writing your paragraph. You would use appropriate explanations, details, and examples for support.

✳ Examining Paragraphs of Comparison and Contrast

Student Writers

Two Loves: Puppy and True

Jennifer Jeffries

Jennifer Jeffries considered several topics before she selected different kinds of love. Just a bit of freewriting convinced her that she had the information and interest to do a good job. In a psychology course she had recently taken, she had read about and discussed ideas about love.

Topic sentence	Of the many forms of love, the two opposite extremes are puppy love and true love. If love in its fullest form has three parts--passion, intimacy, and commitment--then puppy love and true love could be called
Point	*incomplete* and *complete*, respectively. Passion is common to both. Puppy love couldn't exist without *passion*, hence the word puppy--an immature animal that jumps around excitedly licking somebody's face. A
Subject A	person in puppy love is attracted physically to someone and is constantly aroused.
Subject B	A person in true love is also passionate, but the passion is proportional to other parts of love--and life. True love passion is based on more than physical attraction, though that

should not be discounted. It is with the
Point   intimacy factor that puppy love really begins
Subject A   to differ from true love. Puppy love may
promote a lot of talk, but most of it can be
attributed to the arousal factor. There's no
closeness and depth of shared experience.
Subject B   But with true love there is a genuine
closeness and shared concern for each other
that is supportive and reassuring. That
closeness usually comes from years of shared
experience, which also proves commitment. And
Point   it is just that factor, the commitment, that
is probably the main difference between puppy
Subject A   love and true love. The people in puppy love
may talk about eternity, but their love
hasn't really gotten outside the physical
realm. Their love has not been tested,
whereas those in true love have a proven
Subject B   commitment. True love has survived troubles in
this imperfect world and become stronger. And
it has survived because it has more than the
one dimension. These considerations show that
these two loves are very different, though
puppy love may, with time, become true love.
That possibility doesn't mean that age
necessarily corresponds with one form of
love. A person of any age can, by knowing
passion, intimacy, and commitment, experience

```
true love, but true love is more likely to

develop over a period of time.
```

Exercise 1 Discussion and Critical Thinking

1. Do you agree with Jeffries's decision to use the point-by-point pattern rather than the subject-by-subject one? Why or why not?

2. Jeffries says that puppy love can become true love. Can true love ever become puppy love?

3. Jeffries implies that one is much more likely to fall out of puppy love than true love. Do you agree? Why or why not?

4. How much time is required for true love to develop?

```
    Wives and Mothers in Vietnam and in America

                    Thung Tran
```

Born in Vietnam, Thung Tran emigrated to America as a young girl. After observing her mother make the unsteady transition from Vietnamese woman to American woman, Tran was well qualified to write this comparison-and-contrast paragraph.

```
                  Fleeing from communism, many Vietnamese

              left their country to resettle with their

    Topic     families in the United States. Here they
  sentence
              discovered just how American culture is

              different from Vietnamese culture, especially

      I.      for the women who become wives and mothers.

              In Vietnam, a young girl is educated in

      A.      Confucian theories: "Obey your father as a

              child, and your husband when you get
```

married." Living with her in-laws after

B. marriage, her role is that of child bearer and housekeeper. She has to be a good wife, a good mother, and a good daughter-in-law if she wants to be happy. She is the first to rise and the last to go to bed in a household that includes her husband and his parents. She will seldom make decisions and will

C. always be obedient. She expects her husband to support the family financially, protect her, and help his relatives direct the

II. family. In American society the female has a different pattern of experiences. As a girl

A. she learns to think for herself and develop her talents. After she marries, unlike her

B. Vietnamese counterpart, she is likely to work

C. outside the home. Because she provides a part of the financial support, she expects her husband to share some of the work of raising the children, keeping the house, and maintaining a relationship with the in-laws on both sides, who probably live in a

Concluding sentences separate house. In America, ideally, the wife and mother will probably have more independence in the home and more responsibilities outside the home. In Vietnam the wife may be left with a secure position but few options.

Exercise 2 Discussion and Critical Thinking

1. Has Tran organized her paragraph using a point-by-point or subject-by-subject pattern?

2. List any references to the other side that Tran uses to emphasize her comparison.

3. Does Tran shade the evidence to favor one side? Explain.

4. In ideal circumstances, what advantages does each woman experience?

Professional Writer

Pink Kittens and Blue Spaceships

Alison Lurie

> *What are the sources of gender identity? In this passage from her book* The Language of Clothes, *Alison Lurie shows that people condition children from birth.*

In early childhood girls' and boys' clothes are often identical in cut and fabric, as if in recognition of the fact that their bodies are much alike. But the T-shirts, pull-on slacks and zip jackets intended for boys are usually made in darker colors (especially forest green, navy, red and brown) and printed with designs involving sports, transportation and cute wild animals. Girls' clothes are made in paler colors (especially pink, yellow and green) and decorated with flowers and cute domestic animals. The suggestion is that the boy will play vigorously and travel over long distances; the girl will stay home and nurture plants and small mammals. Alternatively, these designs may symbolize their wearers: the boy is a cuddly bear or a smiling tiger, the girl a flower or a kitten. There is also a tendency for boys' clothes to be fullest at the shoulders and girls' at the hips, anticipating their adult figures. Boys' and men's garments also emphasize the shoulders with horizontal stripes, epaulets or yokes of contrasting color. Girls' and women's garments emphasize the hips and rear through the strategic placement of gathers and trimmings.

Exercise 3 Discussion and Critical Thinking

1. Does this paragraph stress comparison or contrast?

2. Is the purpose mainly to inform, to persuade, or to do both?

3. What are the two main points used for comparing and contrasting girls' and boys' clothes?

4. Does Lurie use a point-by-point or a subject-by-subject comparison?

✳ Practicing Patterns of Comparison and Contrast

Exercise 4 Completing Patterns

Fill in the blanks in the following outlines to complete the comparisons and contrasts.

1. Friends: Marla and Justine (subject-by-subject)

    I. Marla

       A. Appearance

       B. _____

       C. _____

   II. Justine

       A. _____

       B. Personality

       C. _____

2. Two Bosses: Mr. Santo and Ms. Elliott (point-by-point)

   I. Disposition

     A. Mr. Santo

     B. Ms. Elliott

  II. Knowledge of _____

     A. _____

     B. Ms. Elliott

 III. _____

     A. Mr. Santo

     B. _____

✳ Topics for Paragraphs of Comparison and Contrast

Reading-Related Topics

"Two Loves: Puppy and True"

1. Using this paragraph as a model, write a comparison-and-contrast piece on two couples you know who are in love.
2. Write a comparative study of two other kinds of love, such as those based mostly on companionship and those based mostly on romance. You could use the same points that Jeffries does: passion, intimacy, and commitment.

"Wives and Mothers in Vietnam and in America"

3. Using this paragraph as a model, compare and contrast students, military personnel, specific professionals, or the disabled in different societies or countries. Begin with whatever they have in common and then discuss how their situations are different. You might want instead to consider two different groups of one society: generations, social classes, and so on. As you compare and contrast, keep in mind that you are generalizing and that individuals differ within groups—avoid stereotyping.

"Pink Kittens and Blue Spaceships"

4. Compare and contrast the toys traditionally given to boys and girls.
5. Compare and contrast the games or recreation generally made available to girls and boys.

Cross-Curricular Topics

6. In the fields of nutritional science and health, compare and contrast two diets, two exercise programs, or two pieces of exercise equipment.
7. Compare and contrast your field of study (or one aspect of it) as it existed some time ago (specify the years) and as it is now. Refer to new developments and discoveries, such as scientific breakthroughs and technological advances.

Career-Related Topics

8. Compare and contrast two products or services, with the purpose of showing that one is better.
9. Compare and contrast two management styles or two working styles.
10. Compare and contrast two career fields to show that one is better for you.
11. Compare and contrast a public school and a business.
12. Compare and contrast an athletic team and a business.

General Topics

The following topics refer to general subjects. Provide specific names and other detailed information as you develop your ideas by using the 4 *P*'s (purpose, points, patterns, and presentation).

13. Two automobiles
14. Two fast-food restaurants
15. Two homes
16. Two people who play the same sport
17. Two generations
18. Two motorcycles, cars, or snowmobiles
19. Two actors, singers, or musicians
20. Two ways of learning
21. Two ways of controlling
22. Two kinds of child care
23. Two mothers: one who stays at home and one who works outside the home

✳ Writer's Guidelines at a Glance: Comparison and Contrast

1. Work with the 4 *P*'s:

   - **Purpose:** Decide whether you want to inform (show relationships) or to persuade (show that one side is better).
   - **Points:** Decide which ideas you will apply to each side. Consider beginning by making a list from which to select.
   - **Patterns:** Decide whether to use subject-by-subject or point-by-point organization.
   - **Presentation:** Decide to what extent you should develop your ideas. Be sure to use cross-references to make connections and to use examples and details to support your views.

2. Your basic subject-by-subject outline will probably look like this:

   I. Subject 1
      A. Point 1
      B. Point 2
   II. Subject 2
      A. Point 1
      B. Point 2

3. Your basic point-by-point outline will probably look like this:

   I. Point 1
      A. Subject 1
      B. Subject 2
   II. Point 2
      A. Subject 1
      B. Subject 2

Definition: Clarifying Terms

✳ Writing Paragraphs of Definition

Most definitions are short; they consist of a **synonym** (a word that has the same meaning as the term to be defined), a phrase, or a sentence. For example, we might say that a hypocrite is a person "professing beliefs or virtues he or she does not possess." Terms can also be defined by **etymology,** or word history. *Hypocrite* once meant "actor" (*hypocrites*) in Greek because an actor was pretending to be someone else. We may find this information interesting and revealing, but the history of a word may be of no use because the meaning has changed drastically over the years. Sometimes definitions occupy a paragraph or an entire essay. The short definition is called a **simple definition;** the longer one is known as an **extended definition.**

Techniques for Development

Paragraphs of definition can take many forms. Among the more common techniques for writing a paragraph of definition are the patterns we have worked with in previous chapters. Consider each of those patterns when you need to write an extended definition. For a particular term, some forms will be more useful than others; use the pattern that best fulfills your purpose.

Each of the following questions takes a pattern of writing and directs it toward definition.

- **Narration:** Can I tell an anecdote or a story to define this subject (such as *jerk, humanitarian,* or *patriot*)? This form may overlap with description and exemplification.
- **Description:** Can I describe this subject (such as *a whale* or *the moon*)?
- **Exemplification:** Can I give examples of this subject (such as naming individuals to provide examples of *actors, diplomats,* or *satirists*)?

- **Analysis by division:** Can I divide this subject into parts (for example, the parts of a *heart, cell,* or *carburetor*)?
- **Process analysis:** Can I define this subject (such as *lasagna, tornado, hurricane, blood pressure,* or any number of scientific processes) by describing how to make it or how it occurs? Common to the methodology of communicating in science, this approach is sometimes called the "operational definition."
- **Cause and effect:** Can I define this subject (such as *a flood, a drought, a riot,* or *a cancer*) by its causes and effects?
- **Classification:** Can I group this subject (such as kinds of *families, cultures, religions,* or *governments*) into classes?

Subject	Class	Characteristics
A republic	is a form of government	in which power resides in the people (the electorate).

- **Comparison and contrast:** Can I define this subject (such as *extremist* or *patriot*) by explaining what it is similar to and different from? If you are defining *orangutan* to a person who has never heard of one but has heard of the gorilla, then you could make comparison-and-contrast statements. If you want to define *patriot,* then you might want to stress what it is not (the contrast) before you explain what it is: a patriot is not a one-dimensional flag waver, not someone who hates "foreigners" because America is always right and always best.

When you develop ideas for a definition paragraph, use a cluster to consider all the paragraph patterns you have learned. Put a double bubble around the subject to be defined. Then put a single bubble around the paragraph patterns and add appropriate words. If a paragraph pattern is not relevant to what you are defining, leave it blank. If you want to expand your range of information, you could add a bubble for a simple dictionary definition and another for an etymological definition. The bubble cluster on page 142 shows how a term could be defined using different paragraph patterns.

Order

The organization of your extended definition is likely to be one of emphasis, but it may be space or time, depending on the subject material. You may use just one pattern of development for the overall sequence. Use the principles of organization discussed in previous chapters.

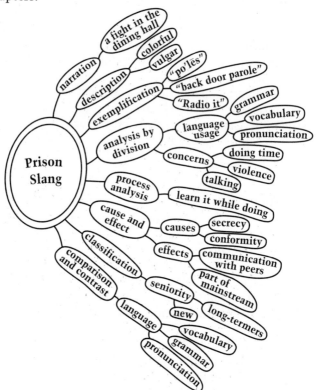

Introduction and Development

Consider these ways of introducing a definition: with a question, with a statement of what it is not, with a statement of what it originally meant, or with a discussion of why a clear definition is important. You may use a combination of these ways or all of them before you continue with your definition.

Development, whether in the form of sentences for the paragraph or of paragraphs for the essay, is likely to represent one or more of the patterns of narration, description, exposition (with its own subdivisions), and argumentation.

Whether you personalize a definition depends on your purpose and your audience. Your instructor may ask you to write about a word within the context of your experience or to write about it from a detached, clinical viewpoint.

✳ Examining Paragraphs of Definition

Student Writers

Going Too Far

Linda Wong

After hearing people say, "I just can't love him [or her] enough,"
and also "It was too much of a good thing," Linda Wong set out to
explore the definition of the word extremist.

<table>
<tr>
<td></td>
<td>Some people believe that it is good to be</td>
</tr>
<tr>
<td></td>
<td>an extremist in some areas, but those people</td>
</tr>
<tr>
<td>What the
term does not
mean</td>
<td>are actually changing the meaning of the word.</td>
</tr>
<tr>
<td></td>
<td>According to the <u>Random House Dictionary of</u></td>
</tr>
<tr>
<td>Simple
definition</td>
<td><u>the English Language</u>, the word extremism</td>
</tr>
<tr>
<td></td>
<td>itself means "excessively biased ideas,</td>
</tr>
<tr>
<td>Topic
sentence</td>
<td>intemperate conduct." <u>The extremist goes too</u></td>
</tr>
<tr>
<td></td>
<td><u>far; that means going too far in whatever the</u></td>
</tr>
<tr>
<td></td>
<td><u>person is doing.</u> I once heard someone say that</td>
</tr>
<tr>
<td></td>
<td>it is good for people to be extremists in</td>
</tr>
<tr>
<td>Example/
contrast</td>
<td>love. But that is not true. <u>It is good to be</u></td>
</tr>
<tr>
<td></td>
<td><u>enthusiastically and sincerely in love, but</u></td>
</tr>
<tr>
<td></td>
<td><u>extremists in love love excessively and</u></td>
</tr>
<tr>
<td></td>
<td><u>intemperately.</u> People who love well may be</td>
</tr>
<tr>
<td></td>
<td>tender and sensitive and attentive, but</td>
</tr>
<tr>
<td></td>
<td>extremists are possessive or smothering.</td>
</tr>
<tr>
<td>Example/
contrast</td>
<td>The same can be said of parents. <u>We all want</u></td>
</tr>
<tr>
<td></td>
<td><u>to be good parents, but parental extremists</u></td>
</tr>
<tr>
<td></td>
<td><u>involve themselves too much in the lives of</u></td>
</tr>
<tr>
<td></td>
<td><u>their children</u>, who, in turn, may find it</td>
</tr>
<tr>
<td></td>
<td>difficult to develop as individuals and become</td>
</tr>
</table>

independent. Even in patriotism, good patriots
are to be distinguished from extreme patriots.

Example/
contrast

Good patriots love their country, but extreme
patriots love their country so much that they
think citizens from other countries are
inferior and suspect. Extreme patriots may
have Hitler-like tendencies. Just what is
wrong with extremists then? It is the loss of

Examples

perspective. The extremists are so preoccupied
with one concern that they lose their sense
of balance. They are the workaholics, the
zealots, the superpatriots of the world.
They may begin with a good objective, but
they focus on it so much that they can become
destructive, obnoxious, and often pitiful. The

Effect and
concluding
sentence

worst effect is that these extremists lose
their completeness as human beings.

Exercise 1   Discussion and Critical Thinking

1. Wong says that extremists "can become destructive, obnoxious,
   and often pitiful." Can you think of any good effects from people
   who were extremists? For example, what about a scientist who
   works fifteen hours a day to find a cure for a horrible disease? Is
   it possible that the scientist may succeed in his or her profession
   and fail in his or her personal life? But what if the scientist does
   not want a personal life? Discuss.

2. Why does Wong use contrast so much?

3. According to Wong, is it bad for a person to be an extremist in religion? Discuss.

Street Cop

Jerry Price

In defining "street cop," student Jerry Price presents a list of his experiences from fifteen years as a police officer in a Los Angeles County community.

Unless you have interviewed a rape victim; have seen the face of family members looking inside their burgled and vandalized home; have driven home a person who has just been carjacked; have told a family that one of their loved ones has died in an accident or has been murdered; have seen a toddler being pulled from the bottom of a pool; have seen a person who has shot himself in the head or hanged himself; have helped a small child find his or her mother; have revived a person using CPR; have been called names and threatened by gang members after telling them to leave a family park as enforcement of a community ordinance; have helped a person with a disabled car; have been thanked by a family for mediating their domestic problems; have been kissed on the cheek by an elderly lady you returned home after she got lost; have been sued in federal court for hitting a

```
felony suspect who was resisting arrest; have
been yelled at for issuing a ticket for
someone going ninety-two miles an hour--
unless you have done these things, you cannot
understand what it is like to be a cop in
these times. It is a definition, a graphic
job description not found in any official
paper. It's just a segment in the life of a
street cop, who is often stereotyped as only
an issuer of traffic tickets.
```

Exercise 2   Discussion and Critical Thinking

1. This definition uses no conventional pattern and has no stated topic sentence. What is the unstated topic sentence?

2. What is the effect of using one exceedingly long sentence to develop the definition?

3. What pattern of development other than definition is used in this paragraph?

4. What does this definition do that an official job description would not do?

Professional Writers

Tornado

Morris Tepper

A tornado may be identified as a particular kind of whirling, highly destructive windstorm. Morris Tepper extends his defini-

tion so that readers will have a good understanding of the many facets of this phenomenon.

What exactly is a tornado? The general picture is familiar enough. The phenomenon is usually brewed on a hot, sticky day with south winds and an ominous sky. From the base of a thundercloud a funnel-shaped cloud extends a violently twisting spout toward the earth. As it sucks in matter in its path, the twister may turn black, brown or occasionally even white (over snow). The moving cloud shows an almost continuous display of sheet lightning. It lurches along in a meandering path, usually northeastward, at 25 to 40 miles per hour. Sometimes it picks up its finger from the earth for a short distance and then plants it down again. The funnel is very slender: its wake of violence generally averages no more than 400 yards wide. As the tornado approaches, it is heralded by a roar of hundreds of jet planes or thousands of railroad cars. Its path is a path of total destruction. Buildings literally explode as they are sucked by the tornado's low-pressure vortex (where the pressure drop is as much as 10 percent) and by its powerful whirling winds (estimated at up to 500 miles per hour). The amount of damage depends mainly on whether the storm happens to hit populated areas. The worst tornado on record in the U.S. was one that ripped across Missouri, lower Illinois and Indiana in three hours on March 18, 1925, and killed 689 people. The tornado's lifetime is as brief as it is violent. Within a few tens of miles (average: about 16 miles) it spends its force and suddenly disappears.

Exercise 3   Discussion and Critical Thinking

1. Which sentence carries the most basic definition of a tornado?

2. Which two paragraph patterns are used throughout this definition?

3. Which pattern is used more?

Burnout

Gregory Moorhead and Ricky W. Griffin

Occupational sociologists Gregory Moorhead and Ricky W. Griffin provide the following definition of burnout *adapted from their book* Organizational Behavior *(2001). Their definition pertains mainly to vocational work, but burnout can occur in any organization—church, government, recreation, even marriage and family.*

Burnout, a consequence of stress, has clear implications for both people and organizations. Burnout is a general feeling of exhaustion that develops when a person simultaneously experiences too much pressure and has too few sources of satisfaction. Burnout usually develops in the following way. First, people with high aspirations and strong motivation to get things done are prime candidates for burnout under certain conditions. They are especially vulnerable when the organization suppresses or limits their initiative while constantly demanding that they serve the organization's own ends. In such a situation, the individual is likely to put too much of himself or herself into the job. In other words, the person may well keep trying to meet his or her own agenda while simultaneously trying to fulfill the organization's expectations. The most likely effects of this situation are prolonged stress, fatigue, frustration, and helplessness under the burden of overwhelming demands. The person literally exhausts his or her aspiration and motivation, much as a candle burns itself out. Loss of self-confidence and psychological withdrawal follow. Ultimately, burnout results. At this point, the individual may start dreading going to work in the morning, may put in longer hours but accomplish less than before, and may generally display mental and physical exhaustion.

Exercise 4   Discussion and Critical Thinking

1. Underline the sentence that best conveys the basic definition.

2. What other pattern—comparison and contrast, classification, cause and effect, or narration—provides structure for this definition?

3. If you were going to personalize this definition, what other pattern would you use?

✳ Practicing Patterns of Definition

Exercise 5 Completing Patterns

Fill in the double bubble with a term to be defined. You might want to define a term like culturally diverse society, educated person, leader, role model, friend, puppy love, true love, success, *or*

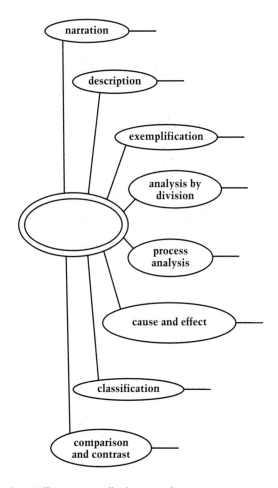

intelligence. *Then fill in at least one more bubble on the right for each paragraph pattern. If the pattern does not apply (that is, if it would not provide useful information for your definition), mark it NA ("not applicable").*

✳ Topics for Paragraphs of Definition

Reading-Related Topics

"Going Too Far"

1. Apply the definition of *extremist* from Linda Wong's paragraph to a situation you are familiar with: an overprotective parent, a controlling companion, an overly controlling boss, a too strict police officer or teacher, a too virtuous friend, a preacher, a too-clean housekeeper (companion, parent), a zealous patriot, a person fanatical about a diet, a person concerned too much with good health or exercise. You might begin your paragraph with the statement: "It is good to be _____, but when _____ is carried to the extreme, the result is _____ ."

"Street Cop"

2. Using this paragraph as a model, define the role or job of someone you know, perhaps yourself. The person might be a daycare worker, security guard, preacher, nurse, firefighter, parent or stepparent, or coach. Keep in mind that the extremely long sentence Price uses is unconventional and should be used only for a special effect.

"Tornado"

3. Define another natural disaster, such as a flood, hurricane, drought, dust storm, or earthquake.
4. Define a natural process, such as oxidation, erosion, photosynthesis, or digestion.

"Burnout"

5. Borrow the definition from this passage and develop it with an extended example of someone you know who is or was a burnout.

Cross-Curricular Topics

Define one of the following terms in a paragraph.

6. History and government: socialism, democracy, patriotism, capitalism, communism.
7. Philosophy: existentialism, free will, determinism, ethics, stoicism.
8. Education: charter schools, school choice, gifted program, ESL, paired teaching, digital school.
9. Music: symphony, sonata, orchestra, tonic systems.
10. Health science: autism, circulatory system, respiratory system, thyroid, cancer, herbal remedies, acupuncture.
11. Marketing: depression, digitalization, discretionary income, electronic commerce, globalization, marketing channel, free trade, telemarketing, warehouse clubs.

Career-Related Topics

12. Define one of the following terms by using the appropriate pattern(s) of development (such as exemplification, cause and effect, narration, comparison and contrast, description, analysis by division, process analysis, and classification): *total quality management, quality control, downsizing, outsourcing, business ethics, customer satisfaction, cost effectiveness.*

General Topics

13. Write a paragraph of extended definition about one of these terms:

Workaholic	Politician
Sexist	Liberated woman
Sexual harassment	Hacker
Macho	Fast food
Soul food	Rap music
Rock music	Street smart
Common sense	Greed
Family	Ecology

✳ Writer's Guidelines at a Glance: Definition

1. Use clustering to consider other patterns of development that may be used to define your term.

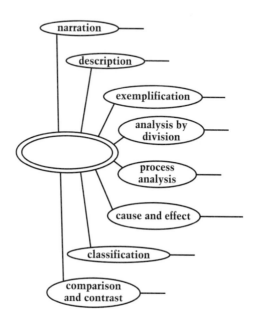

2. The organization of your extended definition is likely to be one of emphasis, but it may be space or time, depending on the subject material. You may use just one pattern of development for the overall organization.
3. Consider these ways of introducing a definition: with a question, with a statement of what it is not, with a statement of what it originally meant, or with a discussion of why a clear definition is important. You may use a combination of these ways before you continue with your definition.
4. Whether you personalize a definition depends on your purpose and your audience. Your instructor may ask you to write about a word within the context of your own experience or to write about it from a detached, clinical viewpoint.

✳ 13

Argument: Writing to Influence

✳ Writing Paragraphs of Argument

Persuasion and Argument Defined

Persuasion is a broad term; when we persuade, we try to influence people to think in a certain way or to do something. **Argument** is persuasion on a topic about which reasonable people disagree. Argument involves controversy. Whereas exercising appropriately is probably not controversial because reasonable people do not dispute the idea, an issue such as gun control is. In this chapter we will be concerned mainly with the kind of persuasion that involves argument.

Components of Your Paragraph

Statements of argument are informal or formal in design. Although an opinion column in a newspaper is likely to have little set structure, an argument in college writing is likely to be tightly organized. Nevertheless, the opinion column and the college paper have much in common. Both provide a proposition, which is the main point of the argument, and both provide support, which is the evidence or the reasons that back up the proposition.

For a well-structured paragraph, an organizational plan is desirable. Consider these elements—background, proposition, qualification of proposition, refutation, and support—when you write a paragraph of argument, and ask yourself the following questions as you develop your ideas:

- **Background:** What is the historical or social context for this controversial issue?
- **Proposition** (the **topic sentence** of a paragraph of argument): What do I want my audience to believe or to do?
- **Qualification of proposition:** Can I limit my proposition so that those who disagree cannot easily challenge me with exceptions? If, for example, I am in favor of using animals for scientific experimentation, am I concerned only with medical exper-

iments or with any use, including that pertaining to the cosmetic industry?

- **Refutation** (taking the opposing view into account, mainly to point out its fundamental weakness): What is the view on the other side, and why is it flawed in reasoning or evidence?
- **Support:** In addition to sound reasoning, can I use appropriate facts, examples, statistics, and opinions of authorities?

The basic form for a paragraph of argument includes the proposition (the topic sentence) and support. The support sentences are, in effect, *because* statements; that is, the proposition is valid *because* of the support. Your organization should look something like this.

> Proposition (topic sentence): It is time to pass a national law restricting smoking in public places.
>
>   I. Discomfort of the nonsmoker (support 1)
>   II. Health of the nonsmoker (support 2)
>   III. Cost to the nation (support 3)

Kinds of Evidence

In addition to sound reasoning, you can use the following kinds of evidence, or support.

1. **Facts.** Martin Luther King Jr. was killed in Memphis, Tennessee, on April 4, 1968. Because an event that has happened is true and can be verified, this statement about King is a fact. But that James Earl Ray acted alone in killing King is to some a questionable fact. That King was the greatest of all civil rights leaders is also opinion because it cannot be verified.

    Some facts are readily accepted because they are general knowledge—you and your reader know them to be true because they can be or have been verified. Other "facts" are based on personal observation and are reported in various publications but may be false or questionable. You should always be concerned about the reliability of the source for both the information you use and the information used by those with other viewpoints. Still other so-called facts are genuinely debatable because of their complexity or the incompleteness of the knowledge available.

2. **Examples.** You must present a sufficient number of examples, and the examples must be relevant.

3. **Statistics.** Statistics are facts and data of a numerical kind that are classified and tabulated to present significant information about a given subject.

   Avoid presenting a long list of figures; select statistics carefully and relate them to things familiar to your reader. The millions of dollars spent on a war in a single week, for example, become more comprehensible when expressed in terms of what the money would purchase in education, highways, or urban renewal.

   To test the validity of statistics, either yours or your opponent's, ask: Who gathered them? Under what conditions? For what purpose? How are they used?

4. **Evidence from, and opinions of, authorities.** Most readers accept facts from recognized, reliable sources—governmental publications, standard reference works, and books and periodicals published by established firms. In addition, they will accept evidence and opinions from individuals who, because of their knowledge and experience, are recognized as experts.

   In using authoritative sources as proof, keep these points in mind:

   - Select authorities who are generally recognized as experts in their field.
   - Use authorities who qualify in the field pertinent to your argument.
   - Select authorities whose views are not biased.
   - Try to use several authorities.
   - Identify an authority's credentials clearly in your paragraph.

✳ Examining Paragraphs of Argument

Student Writer

My Life to Live--or Not

Angela DeSarro

After Angela DeSarro received a list of topics from which to select, she went to the library to obtain some information about the ones that interested her. One such topic was euthanasia. Her electronic data bank offered her an essay in the Journal of the American Medical Association *about a doctor who illegally assisted a suffering, terminally ill patient. DeSarro's mind and emotions came together on the issue and she had her topic.*

Debbie, 20, was dying of ovarian cancer. Racked with pain, nauseous, emaciated, she sought the ultimate relief and found it in euthanasia. A doctor administered a drug and she died. It was a hidden, secret act. It was also illegal in Debbie's state, but this case was written up in the *Journal of the American Medical Association.*

Proposition Surely the time has come for a nationwide law legalizing this practice under specific provisions and regulations.

Support Debbie had reached the point of not only enduring terrible pain but of vomiting constantly and not being able to sleep. Pain-killing medication no longer worked. She wanted to die with what she regarded as a degree of dignity. She had already become a withered, suffering human being with tubes coming out of her nose, throat, and urinary tract, and she was losing all self-control.

Support She also believed that it should be up to her, under these conditions, to decide when and how she should die. Laws in most places prohibit terminally ill patients from choosing death and physicians from assisting them. One state, Oregon, has a law favoring

	physician-assisted suicide, at least in the
	limited cases of terminally ill people
	expected to live less than six months. In
Concluding	1998, fifteen people benefited from that law;
sentence as a	it was not abused. It, or a similar form,
restated	
proposition	should be enacted nationwide.

Exercise 1 Discussion and Critical Thinking

1. What kinds of evidence does DeSarro use to support her argument?

2. What might be the objections to her reasoned argument?

3. Do you agree or disagree with DeSarro's argument? Why?

Professional Writer

The High Price of Steroid Studliness

Anastasia Toufexis

Young men take steroids because they want the Rambo look. However, as Time *magazine writer Anastasia Toufexis points out, they get much more than muscles in their steroids-effects package—and what they get, no one wants.*

Drug-enhanced physiques are a hazardous bargain. Steroids can cause temporary acne and balding, upset hormonal production and damage the heart and kidneys. Doctors suspect they may contribute to liver cancer and atherosclerosis. Teens, who are already undergoing physical and psychological stresses, may run some enhanced risks. The drugs can stunt growth by accelerating bone maturation. Physicians also speculate that the chemicals may compromise youngsters' still developing reproductive systems. Steroid users have experienced a shrinking of the testicles and impotence. Dr. Richard Dominguez, a sports specialist in suburban Chicago, starts his lectures to youths with a surefire attention grabber: "You want to shrink your balls? Take steroids." Just as worrisome is the threat to mental health. Drug users are prone to moodiness, depression, irritability and what are known as "roid rages." Ex-user Darren Allen Chamberlain, 26, of Pasadena, Calif., describes himself as an "easy-going guy" before picking up steroids at age 16. Then he turned into a teen Terminator.

Exercise 2   Discussion and Critical Thinking

1. What is the proposition?

2. What other pattern of development is used for support?

3. About how many effects or possible effects are presented?

4. What is the relevance of this topic?

5. This paragraph is concerned mainly with the effects of steroids on teens. Why do role models, such as athletes, take steroids, even though they know the risks? Why do some teens take steroids?

✳ Practicing Patterns of Argument

Exercise 3   Completing Patterns

Fill in the blanks in the following outlines with supporting statements for each proposition. Each outline uses this pattern:

> Proposition
>   I. Support
>   II. Support
> III. Support

1. Proposition: College athletes should be paid.
   I. _____
   II. They work long hours in practice and competition.
   III. They have less time than many other students for study.
2. Proposition: Zoos are beneficial institutions.
   I. _____
   II. They preserve endangered species by captive breeding.
   III. They study animal diseases and find cures.

✳ Topics for Paragraphs of Argument

Reading-Related Topics

"My Life to Live—or Not"

1. Write an argument in which you agree or disagree with De-Sarro. Incorporate your own value system, religious or secular, into your discussion.
2. Use the Internet or the library to research the state law in Oregon that permits doctors to assist in suicides under certain conditions. Discuss how well the law has worked and whether it should be enacted as a national law or a law in other states.

"The High Price of Steroid Studliness"

3. Using this paragraph as a model, write about why one should not use other drugs (or other families of drugs), including alcohol and nicotine, because of harmful physical and psychological effects.

Cross-Curricular Topics

4. From a class you are taking or have taken, or from your major area of study, select an issue on which thoughtful people may disagree, and write an essay of persuasion or argument. It could be an interpretation of an ambiguous piece of literature for an English class; a position on global warming, public land management, or the Endangered Species Act for a class in ecology; a paper arguing about the effectiveness of a government program in a political-science class; a view on a certain kind of diet in a

food-science class; a preference for a particular worldview in a class on philosophy; or an assertion on the proper role of chiropractors as health-care practitioners in a health-science class.

Career-Related Topics

5. Write a persuasive paragraph in which you argue to solve a problem pertaining to one of the following workplace issues:

   ■ Time-saving equipment
   ■ Doing your job (or part of it) at home rather than at the workplace
   ■ Fringe benefits
   ■ Evaluation procedures
   ■ Staggering lunch hours and work breaks
   ■ Communication between workers on different shifts

General Topics

Write a paragraph on one of the following broad subject areas. You will have to limit your focus for a paragraph of argument. You may also modify the topics to fit specific situations.

6. Banning pit bulls
7. School dress codes
8. School uniforms
9. Sex education
10. Sexual harassment
11. Changing the juvenile-justice system
12. Endangered-species legislation
13. Advertising tobacco
14. Combatting homelessness
15. State-run lotteries
16. Jury reform
17. Legalizing prostitution
18. Censoring rap or rock music
19. Cost of illegal immigration
20. Installation of local traffic signs
21. Foot patrols by local police
22. Change in (your) college registration procedure
23. Local rapid transit
24. Surveillance by video (on campus, in neighborhoods, or in shopping areas)

25. Zone changes for stores selling liquor
26. Curfew for teenagers
27. Laws keeping known gang members out of parks

✳ Writer's Guidelines at a Glance: Argument

1. Consider which aspects of the formal argument you need for your paragraph:

   - **Background:** What is the historical or social context for this controversial issue?
   - **Proposition** (the **topic sentence**): What do I want my audience to believe or to do?
   - **Qualification of proposition:** Have I limited my proposition so that those who disagree with me cannot easily challenge me with exceptions?
   - **Refutation** (taking the opposing view into account, mainly to point out its fundamental weakness): What is the view on the other side, and why is it flawed in reasoning or evidence?
   - **Support:** In addition to sound reasoning, have I used appropriate facts, examples, statistics, and opinions of authorities?

2. The basic pattern of a paragraph of argument is likely to be in this form:

   Proposition (the topic sentence)
   I. Support 1
   II. Support 2
   III. Support 3

✳ 14

✳ From Paragraph to Essay

✳ Writing the Short Essay

The definition of a paragraph gives us a framework for defining the essay: A paragraph is a group of sentences, each with the function of supporting a single, main idea, which is contained in the topic sentence.

The main parts of a paragraph are the topic sentence (subject and treatment), support (evidence and reasoning), and, often, the concluding sentence at the end. Now let's use that framework for an essay: An **essay** is a group of paragraphs, each with the function of stating or supporting a controlling idea called the thesis.

Following are the main parts of the essay:

> **Introduction:** carries the thesis, which states the controlling idea—much like the topic sentence for a paragraph but on a larger scale
> **Development:** evidence and reasoning—the support
> **Conclusion:** an appropriate ending—often a restatement of or a reflection on the thesis

Thus, considered structurally, the paragraph is often an essay in miniature. That does not mean that all paragraphs can grow up to be essays or that all essays can shrink to become paragraphs. For college writing, however, a good understanding of the parallel between well-organized paragraphs and well-organized essays is useful. As you learn the properties of effective paragraphs—those with a strong topic sentence and strong support—you also learn how to organize an essay, if you just magnify the procedure.

The diagram on page 163 illustrates the parallel parts of outlines, paragraphs, and essays:

Of course, the parallel components are not exactly the same in a paragraph and an essay. The paragraph is shorter and requires much

162

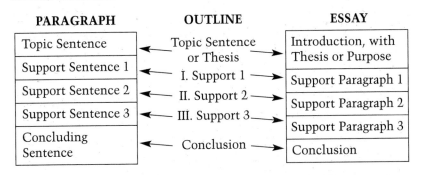

less development, and some paragraph topics simply couldn't be developed much more extensively to their advantage. But let's consider the ones that can. What happens? How do we proceed?

Introductory Paragraph

The topic-sentence idea is expanded to the introductory paragraph through elaboration: explanation, historical background, anecdote, quotation, or stress on the significance of an idea. Usually the introduction is about three to six sentences long. If you say too much, your paper will be top-heavy. If you don't say enough, your readers will be confused. But a solid opening paragraph should

- introduce the subject through the thesis or controlling idea.
- gain reader interest.
- move the reader into the middle paragraphs. You should avoid any statement of apology about your topic or your writing and avoid beginning with a statement like "I am writing an essay about. . . ."

Middle Paragraphs

The middle paragraphs are similar to the paragraphs you have been writing. Each has its own unity based on the topic sentence, moves logically and coherently, and has adequate and appropriate development. The topic sentence is usually at the beginning of the paragraph in a college essay, regardless of the form. Although some essays are an expansion of a particular form of discourse and therefore use basically the same pattern for each paragraph, many essays combine the forms. For example, you might have one middle paragraph that gives examples, one that defines, and one that classifies. You may also have combinations within paragraphs. Nevertheless, the paragraphs are always related to the central idea and presented in a logical arrangement. The coherence of the paragraphs can often be improved by the use of the same principles that you have applied within each paragraph: using sequence words such as *first, second,* and *third;* using transitional words such as *therefore, moreover,* and *for example;* and arranging material in chronological order, spatial order, or order of relative importance.

Concluding Paragraph

Like the introductory paragraph, the concluding paragraph is a special unit with a specific function. In the concluding paragraph, usually three to six sentences long, you end on a note of finality. The way that you end depends on what you want to do. If you can't decide on how to end, try going back to your introduction and see what you said there. If you posed a question, the answer should be in the conclusion. If you laid out the framework for an exploration of the topic, then perhaps you will want to bring your discussion together with a summary statement. Or maybe a quotation, an anecdote, or a restatement of the thesis in slightly different words would be effective. Do not end with a complaint, an apology, or the introduction of a new topic or new support. And do not begin your conclusion with the words such as "last but not least" or "in conclusion." Try for a fresh approach.

✳ Examining a Paragraph and an Essay

Student Writer

The following paragraph and essay, both on the topic of drunk driving, were written by the same student. Notice how each is developed.

Get Them Off the Road (paragraph)

Daniel Humphreys

Topic sentence	<u>Drunk driving has become such a severe problem in California that something must be done.</u> The best solution is to do what Sweden

did long ago: Lower the blood-alcohol content
level to .04 percent for drunk-driving arrests.

I. Support Driving is not a right; it is a privilege, and
that privilege should not be extended to the
person who drinks to the extent that his or her
physical and mental abilities are significantly
impaired. Alcohol, working as a depressant,

II. Support affects our entire nervous system, according to
numerous sources cited in *The Police Officer's
Source Book*. As a result of this impairment,
"50 percent of all fatal traffic accidents"
involve intoxicated drivers, as reported by the
National Highway Traffic Safety Administration.
Cavenaugh and Associates, research specialists,
say that in California 6,863 people were killed
in alcohol-related accidents in the four-year
period from 1997 through 2000. They go on to

III. Support say that nationally intoxicated drivers cost us
somewhere between $11 billion and $14 billion

Concluding each year. It is time to give drunk drivers a
sentence message: "Stay off the road. You are costing us
pain, injury, and death, and no one has the
right to do that."

Get Them Off the Road (essay)

Daniel Humphreys

The state of California, along with the

Introduction rest of the nation, has a problem with

society involving drinking and driving.
Prohibition is not the answer, as history has
demonstrated. But there is a practical answer

Thesis of essay
to be found in a law. <u>I believe that the</u>
<u>legal BAC (blood-alcohol concentration)</u>
<u>while driving should be lowered from .08</u>
<u>percent to .04 percent for three strong</u>
<u>reasons.</u>

Topic sentence of paragraph
First, <u>driving in California is a</u>
<u>privilege</u>, not a right, and <u>a person impaired</u>
<u>by alcohol should not be allowed that</u>
<u>privilege.</u> Statutory law states that when
stopped by a police officer who suspects
drunk driving, one must submit to a BAC test.
The level of impairment is an individual
trait because of the elapsed time of
consumption, body size, and tolerance, but

I. Support paragraph 1
<u>alcohol</u> is a depressant to all of us. It
<u>affects our nervous system and slows our</u>
<u>muscular reactions.</u> As a result of extensive
scientific study, Sweden determined that
.04 percent BAC was the level of significant impairment, and, therefore, it
passed a federal law to enforce drunk
driving at that point. Penalties there are
extreme.

Topic sentence of paragraph
<u>We,</u> like the people in Sweden, <u>are</u>
<u>concerned about the dangers of drunk driving.</u>

**II. Support
paragraph 2**

The National Highway Traffic Safety
Administration has stated that "50 percent of
all fatal accidents" involve intoxicated
drivers and that 75 percent of those drivers
have a BAC of .10 percent or higher.
Cavenaugh and Associates, a California think
tank, reports that in the four-year period
between 1997 and 2000, 17,354 people were
injured and 6,863 were killed in alcohol-
related accidents in California.

**Topic
sentence of
paragraph**

**III. Support
paragraph 3**

Even if we are among the fortunate few
who are not touched directly by the problems
of drunk driving, there are other effects.
One is money. There are the loss of
production, cost of insurance, cost of
delays in traffic, cost of medical care
for those who have no insurance, and many
other costs. Cavenaugh and Associates say
that drunk drivers cost us nationally
somewhere between $11 billion and $14 billion
a year.

Conclusion

**Restated
thesis**

Police officers report that drinking
people are quick to say, "I'm okay to drive,"
but every four years our nation loses more
lives than it lost in the entire Vietnam
War. To lower the legal BAC limit to .04
percent would mean saving lives, property,
and money.

| Exercise 1 | Expanding a Paragraph into an Essay

The following paragraph could easily be expanded into an essay because the topic sentence and its related statements can be developed into an introduction; each of the main divisions (five) can be expanded into a separate paragraph; and the restated topic sentence can, with elaboration, become the concluding paragraph. Divide the following paragraph with the symbol ¶ and annotate it in the left-hand margin with the words Introduction, Support (and numbers for the middle five paragraphs), and Conclusion to show the parts that would be developed further. The topic sentence has already been marked for you.

What Is a Gang?

Will Cusak

<table>
<tr>
<td valign="top">

**Topic
sentence with
related
statements**

</td>
<td>

The word *gang* is often used loosely to
mean "a group of people who go around
together," but that does not satisfy the
concerns of law enforcement people and
sociologists. For these professionals, the
definition of gang has five parts. These five
parts combine to form a unit. First a gang
has to have a name. Some well-known gang
names are Bloods, Crips, Hell's Angels, and
Mexican Mafia. The second part of the
definition is clothing or other identifying
items such as tattoos. The clothing may be of
specific brands or colors, such as blue for
Crips and red for Bloods. Members of the
Aryan Brotherhood often have blue thunderbolt
tattoos. A third component is rituals.
They may involve such things as the use of

</td>
</tr>
</table>

```
handshakes, other body language or signing,

and graffiti. A fourth is binding membership.

A gang member is part of an organization,

a kind of family, with obligations and codes

of behavior to follow. Finally, a gang will

be involved in some criminal behavior,

something such as prostitution, drugs,

thievery, or burglary. There are many

different kinds of gangs--ethnic, regional,

behavioral--but they all have these five

characteristics.
```

☀ Topics for Short Essays

Many paragraph topics in this book can become topics for short essays. Look through the lists of Reading-Related Topics, Career-Related Topics, and General Topics at the end of Chapters 4 through 13 to find ideas that can be expanded. Here are some ways to accomplish the expansion.

Narration: Expand each part of the narrative form (situation, conflict, struggle, outcome, meaning) into one or more paragraphs. Give the most emphasis to the struggle.

Description: Expand each unit of descriptive detail into a paragraph. All paragraphs should support the dominant impression.

Exemplification: Expand one example into an extended example or expand a group of examples into separate paragraphs. Each paragraph should support the main point.

Analysis by division: Expand the discussion by treating each part of the unit in a separate paragraph.

Process analysis: Expand the preparation and each step in the process into a separate paragraph.

Cause and effect: Expand each cause or effect into a separate paragraph.

Classification: Expand each class, or category, into a separate paragraph.

Comparison and contrast: In the point-by-point pattern, expand each point into a separate paragraph.

In the subject-by-subject pattern, first expand each subject into a separate paragraph. If you have sufficient material on each point, you can also expand each point into a separate paragraph.

Definition: Expand each aspect of the definition (characteristics, examples, comparative points) into a separate paragraph.

Argument: Expand the refutation and each main division of support into a separate paragraph.

Of course, the statement that a paragraph is seldom made up of a single pattern also applies to the essay. Most essays have a combination of patterns, although one pattern may prevail and provide the main structure. Therefore, any topic selected from the end-of-chapter suggestions should be developed with an open mind about possibilities of using more than one pattern of development.

✳ Writer's Guidelines at a Glance: From Paragraph to Essay

You do not usually set out to write an essay by first writing a paragraph. But the organization for the paragraph and the essay is often the same, and the writing process is also the same. You still proceed from prewriting to topic, to outline, to draft, to revising, to editing, to final paper. The difference is often only a matter of development and indentation.

1. The well-designed paragraph and the well-designed essay often have the same form.
   a. The **introduction** carries the thesis, which states the controlling idea—much like the topic sentence for a paragraph but on a larger scale.
   b. The development, or middle part, supplies evidence and reasoning—the **support.**
   c. The **conclusion** provides an appropriate ending—often a restatement of, or reflection on, the thesis.

2. The following diagram shows the important relationships among the paragraph, outline, and essay.

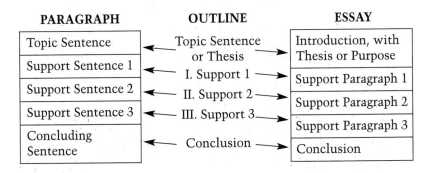

PARAGRAPH	OUTLINE	ESSAY
Topic Sentence	Topic Sentence or Thesis	Introduction, with Thesis or Purpose
Support Sentence 1	I. Support 1	Support Paragraph 1
Support Sentence 2	II. Support 2	Support Paragraph 2
Support Sentence 3	III. Support 3	Support Paragraph 3
Concluding Sentence	Conclusion	Conclusion

✳ Handbook

This handbook presents rules, examples, and exercises for grammar, usage, punctuation, capitalization, spelling, and ESL matters.

✳ Identifying Parts of Speech

To classify a word as a part of speech, we observe two simple principles:

- The word must be in the context of communication, usually in a sentence.
- We must be able to identify the word with others that have similar characteristics—the eight parts of speech: nouns, pronouns, verbs, adjectives, adverbs, prepositions, conjunctions, or interjections.

The first principle is important because some words can be any of several parts of speech. The word *round,* for example, can function as five:

- I watched the potter *round* the block of clay. (verb)
- I saw her go *round* the corner. (preposition)
- She has a *round* head. (adjective)
- The astronauts watched the world go *round.* (adverb)
- The champ knocked him out in one *round.* (noun)

1. Nouns

a. **Nouns are naming words.** Nouns may name persons, animals, plants, places, things, substances, qualities, or ideas—for example, *Bart, armadillo, Mayberry, tree, rock, cloud, love, ghost, music, virtue.*

b. **Nouns are often pointed out by noun indicators.** These noun indicators—*the, a, an*—signal that a noun is ahead, although there may be words between the indicator and the noun itself.

the slime	*a* werewolf	*an* aardvark
the green slime	*a* hungry werewolf	*an* angry aardvark

2. Pronouns

A **pronoun** is a word that is used in place of a noun.

a. Some pronouns may represent specific persons or things:

I	she	they	you
me	her	them	yourself
myself	herself	themselves	yourselves
it	he	we	who
itself	him	us	whom
that	himself	ourselves	

b. Indefinite pronouns refer to nouns (persons, places, things) in a general way:

each   everyone   nobody   somebody

c. Other pronouns point out particular things:

SINGULAR   *this, that*   PLURAL   *these, those*
             This is my treasure.   *These* are my jewels.
             That is your junk.   *Those* are your trinkets.

d. Still other pronouns introduce questions.

Which is the best CD player?
What are the main ingredients of a Twinkie?

3. Verbs

Verbs show action or express being in relation to the subject of a sentence. They customarily occur in set positions in sentences.

a. **Action verbs** are usually easy to identify.

The aardvark *ate* the crisp, tasty ants. (action verb)
The aardvark *washed* them down with a snoutful of water. (action verb)

b. The **being** verbs are few in number and are also easy to identify. The most common *being* verbs are *is, was, were, are,* and *am.*

Gilligan *is* on an island in the South Pacific. (*being* verb)
I *am* his enthusiastic fan. (*being* verb)

c. The form of a verb expresses its tense, that is, the time of the action or being. The time may be in the present or past.

> Roseanne *sings* "The Star-Spangled Banner." (present)
>
> Roseanne *sang* "The Star-Spangled Banner." (past)

d. One or more **helping verbs** may be used with the main verb to form other tenses. The combination is called a **verb phrase.**

> She *had sung* the song many times in the shower. (Helping verb and main verb indicate a time in the past.)
>
> She *will be singing* the song no more in San Diego. (Helping verbs and main verb indicate a time in the future.)

e. Some helping verbs can be used alone as main verbs: *has, have, had, is, was, were, are,* and *am.* Certain other helping verbs function only as helpers: *will, shall, should,* and *could.*

The most common position for the verb is directly after the subject or after the subject and its modifiers.

> At high noon only two men [subject] *were* on Main Street.
>
> The man with the faster draw [subject and modifiers] *walked* away alone.

4. Adjectives

Adjectives modify nouns and pronouns. Most adjectives answer the questions *What kind? Which one?* and *How many?*

a. Adjectives answering the *What kind?* question are descriptive. They tell the quality, kind, or condition of the nouns or pronouns they modify.

> *red* convertible   *dirty* fork
> *noisy* muffler   *wild* roses
> The rain is *gentle.*   Bob was *tired.*

b. Adjectives answering the *Which one?* question narrow or restrict the meaning of a noun. Some of these are pronouns that become adjectives by function.

> *my* money   *our* ideas   the *other* house
> *this* reason   *these* apples

c. Adjectives answering the *How many?* question are, of course, numbering words.

> *some* people   *each* pet   *few* goals
>
> *three* dollars   *one* glove

d. The words *a, an,* and *the* are adjectives called **articles.** As noun indicators, they point out persons, places, and things.

5. Adverbs

a. **Adverbs** modify verbs, adjectives, and other adverbs. Adverbs answer the questions *How? Where? When?* and *To what degree?*

> Modifying Verbs   They <u>did</u> their work <u>quickly</u>.
>   v   adv
>
> Modifying Adjectives   They were <u>somewhat</u> <u>happy</u>.
>   adv   adj
>
> Modifying Adverbs   He answered <u>very</u> <u>slowly</u>.
>   adv   adv

- Adverbs that answer the *How?* question are concerned with manner or way.

  She ate the snails *hungrily*.

  He snored *noisily*.

- Adverbs that answer the *Where?* question show location.

  They drove *downtown*.

  He stayed *behind*.

  She climbed *upstairs*.

- Adverbs that answer the *When?* question indicate time.

  The ship sailed *yesterday*.

  I expect an answer *soon*.

- Adverbs that answer the *To what degree?* question express extent.

  She is *entirely* correct.

  He was *somewhat* annoyed.

b. Most words ending in *-ly* are adverbs.

> He completed the task <u>skillfully</u>.
>   adv

She answered him <u>courteously.</u>
adv

However, there are a few exceptions.

The house provided a <u>lovely</u> view of the valley.
adj

Your goblin mask is <u>ugly.</u>
adj

6. Prepositions

a. A **preposition** is a word or words that function as a connec-
tive. The preposition connects its object(s) to some other word(s)
in the sentence. A preposition and its object(s)—usually a
noun or pronoun—with modifiers make up a **prepositional
phrase.**

Bart worked <u>against</u> great <u>odds.</u>
prep   object
prepositional phrase

Everyone <u>in</u> his <u>household</u> cheered his effort.
prep   object
prepositional phrase

Following are some of the most common prepositions:

about	before	but	into	past
above	behind	by	like	to
across	below	despite	near	toward
after	beneath	down	of	under
against	beside	for	off	until
among	between	from	on	upon
around	beyond	in	over	with

b. Some prepositions are composed of more than one word and are
constructed using other parts of speech:

according to	as far as	because of	in spite of
ahead of	as well as	in back of	instead of
along with	aside from	in front of	together with

<u>According to</u> the weather <u>report,</u> a storm is forming.
prep   object
prepositional phrase

c. *Caution:* Do not confuse adverbs with prepositions.

> I went *across* slowly. (without an object—adverb)
> I went *across* the field. (with an object—preposition)
> We walked *behind* silently. (without an object—adverb)
> We walked *behind* the mall. (with an object—preposition)

7. Conjunctions

a. A **conjunction** connects and shows a relationship between words, phrases, or clauses. A **phrase** is two or more words acting as a part of speech. A **clause** is a group of words with a subject and a verb. An independent clause can stand by itself: *She plays bass guitar.* A dependent clause cannot stand by itself: *when she plays bass guitar.*

b. The two kinds of conjunctions are coordinating and subordinating.

- **Coordinating conjunctions** connect words, phrases, and clauses of equal rank: noun with noun, adjective with adjective, verb with verb, phrase with phrase, main clause with main clause, and subordinate clause with subordinate clause. The seven common coordinating conjunctions are *for, and, nor, but, or, yet,* and *so.* (They form the acronym FANBOYS.)

> TWO NOUNS: Bring a <u>pencil</u> <u>and</u> some <u>paper</u>.
>   noun conj   noun
> TWO PHRASES: Did she go <u>to the store</u> <u>or</u> <u>to the game</u>?
>   prep phrase conj prep phrase

  Paired conjunctions such as *either/or, neither/nor,* or *both/and* are usually classed as coordinating conjunctions.

> <u>Neither</u> the coach <u>nor</u> the manager was at fault.
>   conj   conj

- **Subordinating conjunctions** connect dependent clauses with main clauses. The most common subordinating conjunctions include the following:

after	because	provided	whenever
although	before	since	where
as	but that	so that	whereas
as if	if	till	wherever
as long as	in order that	until	
as soon as	notwithstanding	when	

If the dependent clause comes *before* the main clause, it is set off by a comma.

Although she was in pain, she stayed in the game.

conj   sub   v

dependent clause

If the dependent clause comes *after* the main clause, it usually is *not* set off by a comma.

She stayed in the game *because* she was needed.

conj   sub   v

dependent clause

Caution: Certain words can function as either conjunctions or prepositions. It is necessary to look ahead to see if the word introduces a clause with a subject and verb—conjunction function— or takes an object—preposition function. Some of the words with two functions are *after, for, since,* and *until.*

> *After* the concert was over, we went home. (clause follows— conjunction)
>
> *After* the concert, we went home. (object follows—preposition)

8. Interjections

a. An **interjection** conveys strong emotion or surprise. When an interjection appears alone, it is usually punctuated with an exclamation mark.

> Wow!   Curses!   Cowabunga!   Yaba dabba do!

b. When an interjection appears as part of a sentence, it is usually followed by a comma.

> Oh, I did not consider that problem.

c. The interjection may sound exciting, but it is seldom appropriate for college writing.

✳ Locating Subjects and Verbs

The **subject** is what the sentence is about, and the **verb** indicates what the subject is doing or is being.

Subjects

You can recognize the **simple subject** by asking *Who?* or *What?* causes the action or expresses the state of being found in the verb.

1. The simple subject and the simple verb can be single or compound.

   My *friend* and *I* have much in common.

   My friend *came* and *left* a present.

2. Although the subject usually appears before the verb, it may follow the verb.

   From tiny acorns grow mighty *oaks.*

3. The **command,** or **imperative, sentence** has a "you" as the implied subject, and no stated subject.

   (You) Read the notes.

4. Be careful not to confuse a subject with an object of a preposition.

   The *foreman* [subject] of the *jury* [object of the preposition] directs discussion.

Verbs

Verbs show action or express being in relation to the subject.

1. **Action verbs** show movement or accomplishment of an idea or a deed.

   He *dropped* the book. (movement)

   He *read* the book. (accomplishment)

2. ***Being* verbs** indicate existence.

   They *were* concerned.

3. Verbs may appear as single words or as phrases.

   He *led* the charge. (single word)

   She *is leading* the charge. (phrase)

4. Verbs that are joined by a coordinating conjunction such as *and* and *or* are called **compound verbs.**

   She *worked* for twenty-five years and *retired.*

5. Do not confuse verbs with **verbals,** verblike words that function as other parts of speech.

   The bird *singing* [participle acting as an adjective] in the tree is defending its territory.

   Singing [gerund acting as a noun subject] is fun.

   I want *to eat* [infinitive acting as a noun object].

6. Do not confuse **adverbs** such as *never, not,* and *hardly* with verbs; they only modify verbs.

7. Do not overlook a part of the verb that is separated from another in a question.

   Where *had* the defendant *gone* on that fateful night?

✳ Writing Different Kinds of Sentences

On the basis of number and kinds of clauses, sentences may be classified as simple, compound, complex, and compound-complex.

Clauses

1. A **clause** is a group of words with a subject and a verb that functions as a part or all of a complete sentence. There are two kinds of clauses: independent (main) and dependent (subordinate).

2. An **independent (main) clause** is a group of words with a subject and verb that can stand alone and make sense. An independent clause expresses a complete thought by itself and can be written as a separate sentence.

   I have the money.

3. A **dependent clause** is a group of words with a subject and verb that depends on a main clause to give it meaning. The dependent clause functions in the common sentence patterns as a noun, an adjective, or an adverb.

   When I have the money

Kinds of Sentences Defined

Kind	Definition	Example
1. Simple	One independent clause	She did the work well.
2. Compound	Two or more independent clauses	She did the work well, and she was paid well.
3. Complex	One independent clause and one or more dependent clauses	*Because she did the work well,* she was paid well.
4. Compound-Complex	Two or more independent clauses and one or more dependent clauses	*Because she did the work well,* she was paid well, and she was satisfied.

Punctuation

1. Use a comma before a coordinating conjunction (*for, and, nor, but, or, yet, so*) between two independent clauses.

    The movie was good, *but* the tickets were expensive.

2. Use a comma after a dependent clause (beginning with a subordinating conjunction such as *because, although, when, since,* or *before*) that occurs before the main clause.

    When the bus arrived, we quickly boarded.

3. Use a semicolon between two independent clauses in one sentence if there is no coordinating conjunction.

    The bus arrived; we quickly boarded.

4. Use a semicolon before and usually a comma after a conjunctive adverb (such as *however, otherwise, therefore, on the other hand,* and *in fact*), between two independent clauses (no comma after *then, also, now, thus,* and *soon*).

    The Dodgers have not played well this year; *however,* the Giants have won ten games in a row.

    Spring training went well; then the regular baseball season began.

✳ Combining Sentences

Coordination

If you intend to communicate two equally important and closely related ideas, you certainly will want to place them close together, probably in a **compound sentence** (two or more independent clauses).

1. When you combine two sentences by using a coordinating conjunction, drop the period, change the capital letter to a small letter, and insert a comma before the coordinating conjunction.

   He likes your home. He can visit for only three months.

   He likes your home, *but* he can visit for only three months.

2. When you combine two sentences by using a semicolon, replace the period with a semicolon and change the capital letter that begins the second sentence to a small letter. If you wish to use a conjunctive adverb, insert it after the semicolon and usually put a comma after it.

   He likes your home; he can visit for only three months.

   He likes your home; *however,* he can visit for only three months.

Subordination

If you have two ideas that are closely related, but one is secondary or dependent on the other, you may want to use a complex sentence.

   My neighbors are considerate. They never play loud music.

   Because my neighbors are considerate, they never play loud music.

1. If the dependent clause comes *before* the main clause, set it off with a comma.

   Before you dive, be sure there is water in the pool.

2. If the dependent clause comes *after* or *within* the main clause, set it off with a comma only if you use the word *though* or *although,* or if the words are not necessary to convey the basic meaning in the sentence.

   Be sure there is water in the pool *before you dive.*

Coordination and Subordination

At times you may want to show the relationship of three or more ideas within one sentence. If that relationship involves two or more main ideas and one or more supporting ideas, the combination can be stated in a **compound-complex sentence** (two or more independent clauses and one or more dependent clauses).

Before he learned how to operate a computer, he had trouble
                 dependent clause

with his typewritten assignments, but now he produces clean,
     independent clause   independent clause

attractive material.

Use punctuation consistent with that of the compound and complex sentences.

Other Methods of Combining Ideas

1. Simple sentences can often be combined by using a **prepositional phrase,** a preposition followed by a noun or pronoun object.

   Dolly Parton wrote a song about a coat. The coat had many colors.

   Dolly Parton wrote a song about a coat *of many colors.*

2. To combine simple sentences, use an **appositive,** a noun phrase that immediately follows a noun or pronoun and renames it.

   Susan is the leading scorer on the team. Susan is a quick and strong player.

   Susan, *a quick and strong player,* is the leading scorer on the team.

3. Simple sentences can often be combined by dropping a repeated subject in the second sentence.

   Some items are too damaged for recycling. They must be disposed of.

   Some items are too damaged for recycling and must be disposed of.

4. Sentences can be combined by using a **participial phrase,** a group of words that include a participle, which is a verblike word that usually ends in *-ing* or *-ed.*

   John rowed smoothly. He reached the shore.

   Rowing smoothly, John reached the shore.

✳ Variety in Sentences: Types, Order, Length, Beginnings

Do not bother to look for formulas in this section. Variety in sentences may be desirable for its own sake, to avoid dullness.

However, it is more likely you will revise your paragraphs for reasons that make good sense in the context of what you are writing. The following are some of the variations available to you.

Types

You have learned that all four types of sentences are sound. Your task as a writer is to decide which one to use for a particular thought. That decision may not be made until you revise your composition. Then you can choose on the basis of the relationship of ideas:

> **Simple:** a single idea
> **Compound:** two closely related ideas
> **Complex:** one idea more important than the other
> **Compound-Complex:** a combination of compound and complex

These types were all covered in more detail earlier in this handbook (page 181).

Order

You will choose the order of parts and information according to what you want to emphasize. Typically the most emphatic location is at the end of any unit.

Length

Uncluttered and direct, short sentences commonly draw attention. Because that focus occurs only when they stand out from longer sentences, however, you would usually avoid a series of short sentences.

Beginnings

A long series of sentences with each beginning containing a subject followed by a verb may become monotonous. Consider beginning sentences in different ways:

> **With a prepositional phrase:** *In the distance* a dog barked.
> **With a transitional connective (conjunctive adverb) such as *then, however, or therefore:*** *Then* the game was over.
> **With a coordinating conjunction such as *and* or *but*:** *But* no one moved for three minutes.
> **With a dependent clause:** *Although he wanted a new Corvette,* he settled for a used Ford Taurus.
> **With an adverb:** *Carefully* he removed the thorn from the lion's paw.

✳ Correcting Fragments, Comma Splices, and Run-Ons

Fragments

A correct sentence signals completeness. Each complete sentence must have an **independent clause,** meaning a word or a group of words that contains a subject and a verb that can stand alone.

He enrolled for the fall semester.

A **fragment** (a group of words without a subject, without a verb, or without both) signals incompleteness—it doesn't make sense. You would expect the speaker or writer of a fragment to say or write more or to rephrase it.

1. A **dependent clause,** which begins with a subordinating word, cannot stand by itself.

   Because he left.

   When she worked.

   Although they slept.

2. A **verbal phrase,** a **prepositional phrase,** and an **appositive phrase** may carry ideas, but each is incomplete because it lacks a subject and verb.

VERBAL PHRASE	*having studied hard all evening*
SENTENCE	Having studied hard all evening, John decided to retire.
PREPOSITIONAL PHRASE	*in the store*
SENTENCE	She worked in the store.
APPOSITIVE PHRASE	*a successful business*
SENTENCE	Marks Brothers, a successful business, sells clothing.

Comma Splices and Run-Ons

The **comma splice** consists of two independent clauses with only a comma between them.

The weather was disappointing, we canceled the picnic.

A comma by itself cannot join two independent clauses.

The **run-on** differs from the comma splice in only one respect: it has no comma between the independent clauses. Therefore, the run-on is two independent clauses with *nothing* between them.

The weather was disappointing <u>we canceled the picnic.</u>

Independent clauses must be properly connected.

Correct comma splices and run-ons by using a comma and a coordinating conjunction, a subordinating conjunction, or a semicolon, or by making each clause a separate sentence.

1. Use a comma and a **coordinating conjunction** (*for, and, nor, but, or, yet, so*).

   We canceled the picnic, *for* the weather was disappointing.

2. Use a **subordinating conjunction** (such as *because, after, that, when, although, since, how, until, unless, before*) to make one clause dependent.

   Because the weather was disappointing, we canceled the picnic.

3. Use a **semicolon** (with or without a conjunctive adverb such as *however, otherwise, therefore, similarly, hence, on the other hand, then, consequently, also, thus*).

   The weather was disappointing; we canceled the picnic.

   The weather was disappointing; *therefore*, we canceled the picnic.

4. Make each clause a separate sentence. For a comma splice, replace the comma with a period, and begin the second sentence (clause) with a capital letter. For a run-on, insert a period between the two independent clauses and begin the second sentence with a capital letter.

   The weather was disappointing. We canceled the picnic.

✳ Omissions: When Parts Are Missing

Do not omit words that are needed to make your sentences clear and logical. Of the many types of undesirable constructions in which necessary words are omitted, the following are the most common.

1. **Subjects.** Do not omit a necessary subject in a sentence with two verbs.

ILLOGICAL   The cost of the car was $12,000 but would easily last me through college. (subject of last)

LOGICAL   The cost of the car was $12,000, but the car would easily last me through college.

2. **Verbs.** Do not omit verbs that are needed because of a change in the number of the subject or a change of tense.

ILLOGICAL   The bushes were trimmed and the grass mowed.

LOGICAL   The bushes were trimmed, and the grass was mowed.

ILLOGICAL   True honesty always has and always will be admired by most people. (tense)

LOGICAL   True honesty always has been and always will be admired by most people.

3. *That* **as a conjunction.** The conjunction *that* should not be omitted from a dependent clause if there is danger of misreading the sentence.

MISLEADING   We believed Eric, if not stopped, would hurt himself.

CLEAR   We believed that Eric, if not stopped, would hurt himself.

4. **Prepositions.** Do not omit prepositions in idiomatic phrases, in expressions of time, and in parallel phrases.

ILLOGICAL   Weekends the campus is deserted. (time)

LOGICAL   During weekends the campus is deserted.

ILLOGICAL   I have neither love nor patience with untrained dogs. (parallel phrases)

LOGICAL   I have neither love for nor patience with untrained dogs.

ILLOGICAL   Glenda's illness was something we heard only after her recovery.

LOGICAL   Glenda's illness was something we heard about only after her recovery.

✳ Working with Verb Forms

The twelve verb tenses are shown in this section. The irregular verb *drive* is used as the example. (See pages 190–191 for a list of irregular verbs.)

Simple Tenses

Present

I, we, you, they *drive.*
He, she, it *drives.*

May imply
a continuation from
past to future

Past

I, we, you, he, she, it, they *drove.*

Future

I, we, you, he, she, it,
they *will drive.*

Perfect Tenses

Present Perfect

I, we, you, they *have driven.*
He, she, it *has driven.*

Completed recently
in the past, may continue
to the present

Past Perfect

I, we, you, he, she, it, they
had driven.

Completed prior to a
specific time in the past

Future Perfect

I, we, you, he, she, it, they
will have driven.

Will occur at a time
prior to a specific
time in the future

Progressive Tenses

Present Progressive

I *am driving.*
He, she, it *is driving.*
We, you, they *are driving.*

In progress now

Past Progressive

I, he, she, it *was driving.*
We, you, they *were driving.*

In progress in the
past

Future Progressive

I, we, you, he, she, it, they
will be driving.

In progress in the
future

Perfect Progressive Tenses

Present Perfect Progressive

I, we, you, they *have been
driving.*
He, she, it *has been driving.*

In progress up to now

Past Perfect Progressive

I, we, you, he, she, it, they *had been driving.*

In progress before another event in the past

Future Perfect Progressive

I, we, you, he, she, it, they *will have been driving.*

In progress before another event in the future

Past Participles

The past participle uses the helping verbs *has, have,* or *had* along with the past tense of the verb. For regular verbs, whose past tense ends in *-ed,* the past-participle form of the verb is the same as the past tense.

Following is a list of some common regular verbs, showing the base form, the past tense, and the past participle. (The base form can also be used with such helping verbs as *can, could, do, does, did, may, might, must, shall, should, will,* and *would.*)

Regular Verbs

Base Form (Present)	Past	Past Participle
ask	asked	asked
answer	answered	answered
cry	cried	cried
decide	decided	decided
dive	dived (dove)	dived
drag	dragged	dragged
finish	finished	finished
happen	happened	happened
learn	learned	learned
like	liked	liked
love	loved	loved
need	needed	needed
open	opened	opened
start	started	started
suppose	supposed	supposed
walk	walked	walked
want	wanted	wanted

Whereas **regular verbs** are predictable—having an *-ed* ending for past and past-participle forms—**irregular verbs,** as the term suggests, follow no definite pattern.

Following is a list of some common irregular verbs, showing the base form (present), the past tense, and the past participle.

Irregular Verbs

Base Form (Present)	Past	Past Participle
arise	arose	arisen
awake	awoke (awaked)	awaked
be	was, were	been
become	became	become
begin	began	begun
bend	bent	bent
blow	blew	blown
break	broke	broken
bring	brought	brought
buy	bought	bought
catch	caught	caught
choose	chose	chosen
cling	clung	clung
come	came	come
creep	crept	crept
deal	dealt	dealt
do	did	done
drink	drank	drunk
drive	drove	driven
eat	ate	eaten
feel	felt	felt
fight	fought	fought
fling	flung	flung
fly	flew	flown
forget	forgot	forgotten
freeze	froze	frozen
get	got	got (gotten)
go	went	gone
grow	grew	grown
have	had	had
know	knew	known
lead	led	led
leave	left	left
lose	lost	lost

Base Form (Present)	Past	Past Participle
mean	meant	meant
read	read	read
ride	rode	ridden
ring	rang	rung
see	saw	seen
shine	shone	shone
shoot	shot	shot
sing	sang	sung
sink	sank	sunk
sleep	slept	slept
slink	slunk	slunk
speak	spoke	spoken
spend	spent	spent
steal	stole	stolen
stink	stank (stunk)	stunk
sweep	swept	swept
swim	swam	swum
swing	swung	swung
take	took	taken
teach	taught	taught
tear	tore	torn
think	thought	thought
throw	threw	thrown
wake	woke (waked)	woken (waked)
weep	wept	wept
write	wrote	written

"Problem" Verbs

The following pairs of verbs are especially troublesome and confusing: *lie* and *lay, sit* and *set,* and *rise* and *raise.* One way to tell them apart is to remember which word in each pair takes a direct object. A direct object answers the question *whom* or *what* in connection with a verb. The words *lay, raise,* and *set* take a direct object.

He *raised* the window. (He *raised* what?)

Lie, rise, and *sit,* however, cannot take a direct object. We cannot, for example, say "He rose the window." In the following examples, the italicized words are objects.

Present Tense	Meaning	Past Tense	Past Participle	Example
lie	to rest	lay	lain	I lay down to rest.
lay	to place something	laid	laid	We laid the *books* on the table.
rise	to go up	rose	risen	The smoke rose quickly.
raise	to lift	raised	raised	She raised the *question*.
sit	to rest	sat	sat	He sat in the chair.
set	to place something	set	set	They set the *basket* on the floor.

Verb Tense

Verb tense is a word form indicating time. The rules about selecting a **tense** for certain kinds of writing are flexible. You should be consistent, however, changing tense only for a good reason.

Usually you should select the present tense to write about literature.

> Moby Dick *is* a famous white whale.

Select the past tense to write about yourself (usually) or something historical (always).

> I *was* eighteen when I *decided* I *was* ready for independence.

Making Subjects and Verbs Agree

This section is concerned with number agreement between subjects and verbs. The basic principle of **subject-verb agreement** is that if the subject is singular, the verb should be singular, and if the subject is plural, the verb should be plural. There are ten major guidelines. In the examples under the following guidelines, the true subjects and verbs are italicized.

1. Do not let words that come between the subject and verb affect agreement.

   a. Modifying phrases and clauses frequently come between the subject and verb:

      > The various *types* of drama *were* not *discussed.*
      >
      > *Angela,* who is hitting third, *is* the best player.
      >
      > The *price* of those shoes *is* too high.

   b. Certain prepositions can cause trouble. The following words are prepositions, not conjunctions: *along with, as well as, besides, in addition to, including,* and *together with.* The words that function as objects of prepositions cannot also be subjects of the sentence.

The *coach,* along with the players, *protests* the decision.

c. In compound subjects in which one subject is positive and one subject is negative, the verb agrees with the positive subject.

Phillip, not the other boys, *was* the culprit.

2. Do not let inversions (verb before subject, not the normal order) affect the agreement of subject and verb.

a. Verbs and other words may come before the subject. Do not let them affect the agreement. To understand subject-verb relationships, recast the sentence in normal word order.

Are Juan and his *sister* at home? (question form)

Juan and his *sister are* at home. (normal order)

b. A sentence filler is a word that is grammatically independent of other words in the sentence. The most common fillers are *there* and *here.* Even though a sentence filler precedes the verb, it should not be treated as the subject.

There *are* many *reasons* for his poor work. (The verb *are* agrees with the subject reasons.)

3. A singular verb agrees with a singular indefinite pronoun.

a. Most indefinite pronouns are singular.

Each of the women *is* ready at this time.

Neither of the women *is* ready at this time.

One of the children *is* not paying attention.

b. Certain indefinite pronouns do not clearly express either a singular or plural number. Agreement, therefore, depends on the meaning of the sentence. These pronouns are *all, any, none,* and *some.*

All of the melon *was* good.

All of the melons *were* good.

None of the pie *is* acceptable.

None of the pies *are* acceptable.

4. Two or more subjects joined by *and* usually take a plural verb.

> The *captain* and the *sailors were* happy to be ashore.
> The *trees* and *shrubs need* more care.

a. If the parts of a compound subject mean one and the same person or thing, the verb is singular; if the parts mean more than one, the verb is plural.

> The *secretary* and *treasurer is* not present. (one person)
> The *secretary* and the *treasurer are* not present. (more than one person)

b. When *each* or *every* modify singular subjects joined by *and*, the verb is singular.

> Each *boy* and each *girl brings* a donation.
> Every *woman* and *man has asked* the same questions.

5. Alternative subjects—that is, subjects joined by *or, nor, either/or, neither/nor, not only/but also*—should be handled in the following manner.

a. If the subjects are both singular, the verb is singular.

> *Rosa* or *Alicia* is responsible.

b. If the subjects are plural, the verb is plural.

> Neither the *students* nor the *teachers were* impressed by his comments.

c. If one of the subjects is singular and the other subject is plural, the verb agrees with the nearer subject.

> Either the Garcia *boys* or their *father goes* to the hospital each day.
> Either their *father* or the Garcia *boys go* to the hospital each day.

6. Collective nouns—*team, family, group, crew, gang, class, faculty,* and the like—take a singular verb if the verb is considered a unit, but a plural verb if the group is considered as a number of individuals.

> The *team is playing* well tonight.
> The *team are getting* dressed. (Here the individuals are acting not as a unit but separately. If you don't like the way this

sounds, rewrite as "The members of the team are getting dressed.")

7. Titles of books, essays, short stories, and plays, a word spoken of as a word, and the names of businesses take a singular verb.

   The Canterbury Tales was written by Geoffrey Chaucer.

   Markle Brothers has a sale this week.

8. Sums of money, distances, and measurements are followed by a singular verb when a unit is meant. They are followed by a plural verb when the individual elements are considered separately.

   Three dollars was the price. (unit)

   Three dollars were lying there. (individual)

   Five years is a long time. (unit)

   The *first five years were* difficult ones. (individual)

9. Be careful of agreement with nouns ending in -s. Several nouns ending in -s take a singular verb—for example, *aeronautics, civics, economics, ethics, measles,* and *mumps.*

   Mumps is an extremely unpleasant disease.

   Economics is my major field of study.

10. Some nouns have only a plural form and so take only a plural verb—for example, *clothes, fireworks, scissors,* and *pants.*

    His *pants are* badly wrinkled.

    Mary's *clothes were* stylish and expensive.

✳ Giving Verbs Voice

Which of these sentences sounds better to you?

   Ken Griffey Jr. slammed a home run.

   A home run was slammed by Ken Griffey Jr.

Both sentences carry the same message, but the first expresses it more effectively. The subject (*Ken Griffey Jr.*) is the actor. The verb (*slammed*) is the action. The direct object (*home run*) is the receiver of the action. The second sentence lacks the vitality of the first because the receiver of the action is the subject; the doer is embedded in the prepositional phrase at the end of the sentence.

The first sentence demonstrates the active voice. It has an active verb (one that leads to a direct object), and the action moves from the beginning to the end of the sentence. The second exhibits the passive voice (with the action reflecting back on the subject). When given a choice, you should usually select the active voice. It promotes energy and directness.

The passive voice, though not usually the preferred form, does have its uses:

- When the doer of the action is unknown or unimportant

    My car was stolen. (The doer, a thief, is unknown.)

- When the receiver of the action is more important than the doer

    My neighbor was permanently disabled by an irresponsible drunk driver. (The neighbor's suffering is the focus, not the drunk driver.)

As you can see, the passive construction places the doer at the end of a prepositional phrase (as in the second example) or does not include the doer in the statement at all (as in the first example). Instead, the passive voice places the receiver of the action in the subject position, and it presents the verb in its past-tense form preceded by a *to be* helper. The transformation is a simple one:

ACTIVE   She read the book.

PASSIVE   The book was read by her.

Because weak sentences often involve the unnecessary and ineffective use of the passive form, you should learn to identify passive constructions and consider changing them to active.

✳ Selecting Pronoun Case

A **pronoun** is a word that is used in place of a noun. **Case** is the form a pronoun takes as it fills a position in a sentence.

1. **Subjective pronouns** are *I, he,* and *she* (singular), and *we* and *they* (plural). *Who* can be either singular or plural.

    Subjective case pronouns can fill subject positions in a sentence.

    We dance in the park.

    It was *she* who spoke. (referring back to and meaning the same as the subject)

2. **Objective pronouns** are *me, him,* and *her* (singular); and *us* and *them* (plural). *Whom* can be either singular or plural. Objective case pronouns fill object positions.

> We saw *her* in the library. (object of verb)
>
> They gave the results to *us*—Judy and *me.* (object of a preposition)

3. Three techniques are useful for deciding what pronoun case to use.

   a. If you have a compound element (such as a subject or an object of a preposition), consider only the pronoun part.

> They will visit Jim and (I, me). (*Consider:* They will visit *me.*)

   b. If the next important word after *who* or *whom* in a statement is a noun or pronoun, the word choice will be *whom;* otherwise, it will be *who.* Disregard qualifier clauses such as *It seems* and *I feel.*

> The person *who* works hardest will win.
>
> The person *whom* judges like will win.
>
> The person *who,* we think, worked hardest won. (ignoring the qualifier clause)

   c. *Let's* is made up of the words *let* and *us* and means *"you let us"*; therefore, when you select a pronoun to follow it, consider the two original words and select another object word—*me.*

> Let's you and *me* go to town.

❋ Matching Pronouns and Antecedents

A pronoun agrees with its antecedent in person, number, and gender.

1. Avoid needless shifting in **person,** which means shifting in point of view, such as from *I* to *you.*

> INCORRECT   *I* tried but *you* couldn't persuade her to return.
>
> CORRECT   *I* tried but *I* couldn't persuade her to return.

2. Most problems with pronoun-antecedent agreement involve number. The principles are simple: If the antecedent (the word the pronoun refers back to) is singular, use a singular pronoun. If the antecedent is plural, use a plural pronoun.

Jim forgot *his* notebook.

Many students cast *their* votes today.

Someone lost *his* or *her* [not *their*] book.

3. The pronoun should agree with its antecedent in gender, if the gender of the antecedent is specific. Masculine and feminine pronouns are gender-specific: *he, him, she,* and *her.* Others are neuter: *I, we, me, us, it, they, them, who, whom, that,* and *which.* The words *who* and *whom* refer to people. *That* can refer to ideas, things, and people, but usually not to people. *Which* refers to ideas and things, but never to people. To avoid a perceived sex bias, most writers and speakers prefer to use *he or she* or *his or her* instead of just *he* or *his;* however, many writers simply make antecedents plural.

Everyone should work until *he or she* drops.

People should work until *they* drop.

✳ Using Adjectives and Adverbs

1. **Adjectives** modify (describe) nouns and pronouns and answer the questions *Which one? What kind?* and *How many?*
2. **Adverbs** modify verbs, adjectives, or other adverbs and answer the questions *How? Where? When?* and *To what degree?* Most words ending in *-ly* are adverbs.
3. If you settle for a common word such as *good* or a slang word such as *neat* to characterize something you like, you will be limiting your communication. The more precise the word, the better the communication. Keep in mind, however, that anything can be overdone; therefore, use adjectives and adverbs wisely and economically.
4. For making comparisons, most adjectives and adverbs have three different forms: the positive (one), the comparative (two), and the superlative (three or more).

   a. Adjectives

   - Add *-er* to short adjectives (one or two syllables) to rank units of two.

     Julian is *kinder* than Sam.

   - Add *-est* to short adjectives (one or two syllables) to rank units of more than two.

Of the fifty people I know, Julian is the *kindest.*

- Add the word *more* before long adjectives to rank units of two.

    My hometown is *more beautiful* than yours.

- Add the word *most* before long adjectives to rank units of three or more.

    My hometown is the *most beautiful* in all America.

- Some adjectives are irregular in the way they change to show comparison: *good, better, best; bad, worse, worst.*

  b. Adverbs

For most adverbs, use the word *more* before the comparative form (two) and the word *most* before the superlative form (three or more).

Jim performed *skillfully.* (modifier)

Joan performed *more skillfully* than Morton. (comparative modifier)

But Susan performed *most skillfully* of all. (superlative modifier)

5. Avoid double negatives. Words such as *no, not, none, nothing, never, hardly, barely,* and *scarcely* should not be combined.

    INCORRECT I *don't* have *no* time for recreation.

    CORRECT I have *no* time for recreation.

    CORRECT I *don't* have time for recreation.

6. Do not confuse adjectives (*bad*) with adverbs (*badly*).

    INCORRECT I feel *badly* about being late.
    CORRECT I feel *bad* about being late.

    INCORRECT He handled the situation *bad.*
    CORRECT He handled the situation *badly.*

✳ Eliminating Dangling and Misplaced Modifiers

1. A modifier that gives information but doesn't refer to a word or group of words already in the sentence is called a **dangling modifier.**

    DANGLING *Walking down the street,* a snake startled me.

    CORRECT *Walking down the street,* I was startled by a snake.

2. A modifier that is placed so that it modifies the wrong word or words is called a **misplaced modifier.**

> MISPLACED   The sick man went to a doctor *with a high fever.*
>
> CORRECT   The sick man with a high fever went to a doctor.

✳ Balancing Sentence Parts

1. **Parallelism** means balancing one structure with another of the same kind—nouns with nouns, verbs with verbs, adjectives (words that can describe nouns) with adjectives, adverbs (words that can describe verbs) with adverbs, and so forth.

> *Men, women,* and *children* [nouns] *enjoy* the show and *return* [verbs] each year.
>
> She fell *in love* and *out of love* [prepositional phrases] in a few seconds.
>
> *She fell in love with him,* and *he fell in love with her* [clauses].

2. Faulty parallel structure is awkward and draws unfavorable attention to what is being said.

> *To talk* with his buddies and *eating* fast foods were his favorite pastimes. (The sentence should be *Talking . . .* and *eating* or *To talk . . .* and *to eat.*)

3. Some words signal parallel structure. All coordinating conjunctions (*for, and, nor, but, or, yet, so*) can give such signals.

> The weather is hot *and* humid.
>
> He purchased a Dodger Dog, *but* I chose Stadium Peanuts.

4. Combination words also signal the need for parallelism or balance. The most common are *either/or, neither/nor, not only/but also, both/and,* and *whether/or.*

> We will *either* win this game *or* go out fighting. (verb following each of the combination words)

✳ Avoiding Wordy Phrases

Certain phrases clutter sentences, consuming our time in writing and our readers' time in reading. Watch for wordy phrases as you revise and edit.

WORDY *Due to the fact that* he was unemployed, he had to use public transportation.

CONCISE *Because* he was unemployed, he had to use public transportation.

WORDY *Deep down inside* he believed that the Red Sox would win.

CONCISE He believed that the Red Sox would win.

Wordy	Concise
at the present time	now
basic essentials	essentials
blend together	blend
it is clear that	(delete)
due to the fact that	because
for the reason that	because
I felt inside	I felt
in most cases	usually
as a matter of fact	in fact
in the event that	if
until such time as	until
I personally feel	I feel
in this modern world	today
in order to	to
most of the people	most people
along the lines of	like
past experience	experience
at that point in time	then
in the final analysis	finally
in the near future	soon
have a need for	need
in this day and age	now

✳ Mastering Punctuation

1. The three marks of end punctuation are periods, question marks, and exclamation points.

   a. Periods

      Place a period after a statement.
      Place a period after common abbreviations.

Use an ellipsis—three periods within a sentence and four periods at the end of a sentence—to indicate that words have been omitted from quoted material.

> He stopped walking and the buildings . . . rose up out of the misty courtroom. . . . (James Thurber, "The Secret Life of Walter Mitty")

b. Question Marks

Place a question mark at the end of a direct question.
Use a single question mark in sentence constructions that contain a double question—that is, a quoted question following a question.

> Mr. Martin said, "Did he say, 'Are we going?'"

Do *not* use a question mark after an indirect (reported) question.

> She asked me what caused the slide.

c. Exclamation Points

Place an exclamation point after a word or group of words that expresses strong feeling.
Do not overwork the exclamation point. Do not use double exclamation points.

2. The comma is used essentially to separate and to set off sentence elements.

a. Use a comma to separate main clauses joined by one of the coordinating conjunctions—*for, and, nor, but, or, yet, so.*

> We went to the game, *but* it was canceled.

b. Use a comma after introductory dependent clauses and long introductory phrases (generally, four or more words is considered long).

> *Before she and I arrived,* the meeting was called to order.

c. Use a comma to separate words, phrases, and clauses in a series.

> He ran *down the street, across the park,* and *into the arms* of his father.

d. Use a comma to separate coordinate adjectives not joined by *and* that modify the same noun.

I need a *sturdy, reliable* truck.

e. Use a comma to separate sentence elements that might be misread.

> *Inside,* the dog scratched his fleas.

f. Use commas to set off (enclose) nonessential (unnecessary for meaning of the sentence) words, phrases, and clauses.

> Maria, *who studied hard,* will pass.

g. Use commas to set off parenthetical elements such as mild interjections (*oh, well, yes, no,* and others), most conjunctive adverbs (*however, otherwise, therefore, similarly, hence, on the other hand,* and *consequently,* but not *then, thus, soon, now,* and *also*), quotation indicators, and special abbreviations (*etc., i.e., e.g.,* and others).

> *Oh,* what a silly question! (mild interjection)
>
> It is necessary, *of course,* to leave now. (sentence modifier)
>
> We left early; *however,* we missed the train anyway. (conjunctive adverb)
>
> "When I was in school," *he said,* "I read widely." (quotation indicator)
>
> Books, papers, pens, *etc.,* were scattered on the floor. (The abbreviation *etc.,* however, should be used sparingly.)

h. Use commas to set off nouns used as direct address.

> Play it again, *Sam.*

i. Use commas to separate the numbers in a date.

> June *4, 1965,* is a day I will remember.

j. Use commas to separate the city from the state. No comma is used between the state and the ZIP code.

> Walnut, CA 91789

k. Use a comma following the salutation and the complementary closing in a letter (but in a business letter, use a colon after the salutation).

> Dear John,
> Sincerely,

1. Use a comma in numbers to set off groups of three digits. However, omit the comma in dates and in long serial numbers, page numbers, and street numbers.

> The total assets were *$2,000,000.*
>
> I was born in 1980.

3. The semicolon indicates a stronger division than the comma. It is used principally to separate independent clauses within a sentence.

   a. Use a semicolon to separate independent clauses not joined by a coordinating conjunction.

   > You must buy that car today; tomorrow will be too late.

   b. Use a semicolon between two independent clauses joined by a conjunctive adverb (such as *however, otherwise, therefore, similarly, hence, on the other hand, then, consequently, accordingly, thus*).

   > It was very late; *therefore,* I remained at the hotel.

4. Quotation marks bring special attention to words.

   a. Quotation marks are used principally to set off direct quotations. A direct quotation consists of material taken from the written work or the direct speech of others; it is set off by double quotation marks. Single quotation marks are used to set off a quotation within a quotation.

   > He said, "I don't remember if she said, 'Wait for me.'"

   b. Use double quotation marks to set off titles of shorter pieces of writing such as magazine articles, essays, short stories, short poems, one-act plays, chapters in books, songs, and separate pieces of writing published as part of a larger work.

   > The book *Literature: Structure, Sound, and Sense* contains a deeply moving poem titled "On Wenlock Edge."
   >
   > Have you read "The Use of Force," a short story by William Carlos Williams?
   >
   > My favorite Elvis song is "Don't Be Cruel."

   c. Punctuation with quotation marks follows definite rules.

   - A period or comma is always placed *inside* the quotation marks.

Our assignment for Monday was to read Poe's "The Raven."

"I will read you the story," he said. "It is a good one."

- A semicolon or colon is always placed *outside* the quotation marks.

He read Robert Frost's poem "Design"; then he gave the examination.

- A question mark, exclamation point, or dash is placed *outside* the quotation marks when it applies to the entire sentence and *inside* the quotation marks when it applies to the material in quotation marks.

He asked, "Am I responsible for everything?" (quoted question within a statement)

Did you hear him say, "I have the answer"? (statement within a question)

Did she say, "Are we ready?" (question within a question)

She shouted, "Impossible!" (exclamation)

"I hope—that is, I—" he began. (dash)

5. Italics (slanting type) is used to call special attention to certain words or groups of words. In handwriting, such words are underlined.

a. Italicize (underline) foreign words and phrases that are still listed in the dictionary as foreign.

nouveau riche   Weltschmerz

b. Italicize (underline) titles of books (except the Bible), long poems, plays, magazines, motion pictures, musical compositions, newspapers, works of art, names of aircraft, ships, and letters, figures, and words referred to by their own name.

War and Peace   Apollo 12   leaving *o* out of *sophomore*

6. The dash is used when a stronger break than the comma is needed. It can also be used to indicate a break in the flow of thought and to emphasize words (less formal than the colon in this situation).

Here is the true reason—but maybe you don't care.

English, French, history—these are the subjects I like.

7. The colon is a formal mark of punctuation used chiefly to introduce something that is to follow, such as a list, a quotation, or an explanation.

> These cars are my favorites: Cadillac, Chevrolet, Buick, Oldsmobile, and Pontiac.

8. Parentheses are used to set off material that is of relatively little importance to the main thought of the sentence. Such material—numbers that designate items in a series, figures, supplementary material, and sometimes explanatory details—merely amplifies the main thought.

> The years of the era (1961–1973) were full of action.
>
> Her husband (she had been married only a year) died last week.

9. Brackets are used within a quotation to set off editorial additions or corrections made by the person who is quoting.

> Churchill said: "It [the Yalta Agreement] contained many mistakes."

10. The apostrophe is used with nouns and indefinite pronouns to show possession, to show the omission of letters and figures in contractions, and to form the plurals of letters, figures, and words referred to as words.

> man's coat   girls' clothes
>
> you're (contraction of *you are*)   five *and*'s

11. The hyphen brings two or more words together into a single compound word. Correct hyphenation, therefore, is essentially a spelling problem rather than one of punctuation. Because the hyphen is not used with any degree of consistency, consult your dictionary for current usage. Study the following as a beginning guide.

   a. Use a hyphen to separate the parts of many compound words.

   > about-face   go-between

   b. Use a hyphen between prefixes and proper names.

   > all-American   mid-November

   c. Use a hyphen to join two or more words used as a single adjective modifier before a noun.

first-class service   hard-fought game
sad-looking mother

d. Use a hyphen with spelled-out compound numbers up to ninety-nine and with fractions.

twenty-six   two-thirds

Note: Dates, street addresses, numbers requiring more than two words, chapter and page numbers, time followed directly by *a.m.* or *p.m.*, and figures after a dollar sign or before measurement abbreviations are usually written as figures, not words.

❋ Conquering Capitalization

In English, there are many conventions concerning the use of capital letters. Here are some of them.

1. Capitalize the first word of a sentence.
2. Capitalize proper nouns and adjectives derived from proper nouns.

- Names of persons
  Edward Jones
- Adjectives derived from proper nouns
  a Shakespearean sonnet   a Miltonic sonnet
- Countries, nationalities, races, and languages
  Germany   English   Spanish   Chinese
- States, regions, localities, and other geographical divisions
  California   the Far East   the South
- Oceans, lakes, mountains, deserts, streets, and parks
  Lake Superior   Fifth Avenue   Sahara Desert
- Educational institutions, schools, and courses
  Santa Ana College   Spanish 3   Joe Hill School
  Rowland High School
- Organizations and their members
  Boston Red Sox   Boy Scouts   Audubon Society
- Corporations, governmental agencies or departments, trade names
  U.S. Steel Corporation   Treasury Department
  White Memorial Library   Coke
- Calendar references such as holidays, days of the week, months
  Easter   Tuesday   January

- Historic eras, periods, documents, laws
  Declaration of Independence   Geneva Convention
  First Crusade   Romantic Age

3. Capitalize words denoting family relationships when they are used before a name or substituted for a name.

> He walked with his nephew and Aunt Grace.
>
> *but*
>
> He walked with his nephew and his aunt.
>
> Grandmother and Mother are away on vacation.
>
> *but*
>
> My grandmother and my mother are away on vacation.

4. Capitalize abbreviations after names.

> Henry White Jr.   William Green, M.D.

5. Capitalize titles of themes, books, plays, movies, poems, magazines, newspapers, musical compositions, songs, and works of art. Do not capitalize short conjunctions and prepositions unless they come at the beginning or the end of the title.

> *Desire Under the Elms*   *Terminator*
> *Last of the Mohicans*   *Of Mice and Men*
> "Blueberry Hill"

6. Capitalize any title preceding a name or used as a substitute for a name. Do not capitalize a title following a name.

> Judge Stone   Alfred Stone, a judge
> General Clark   Raymond Clark, a general
> Professor Fuentes   Harry Jones, the former president

✳ Index

214